Simon & Schuster

New York   London   Toronto   Sydney   New Delhi

Polish Your Poise with

MADAME

CHIC

Lessons

in

Everyday Elegance

JENNIFER L. SCOTT

Simon & Schuster
1230 Avenue of the Americas
New York, NY 10020

First Simon & Schuster hardcover edition November 2015

SIMON & SCHUSTER and colophon are registered
trademarks of Simon & Schuster, Inc.

For information about special discounts for bulk purchases,
please contact Simon & Schuster Special Sales
at 1-866-506-1949 or business@simonandschuster.com.

The Simon & Schuster Speakers Bureau can bring authors
to your live event. For more information or to book an event, contact the
Simon & Schuster Speakers Bureau at 1-866-248-3049 or
visit our website at www.simonspeakers.com.

Manufactured in the United States of America

10 9 8 7 6 5 4 3 2 1

Library of Congress Cataloging-in-Publication Data
Scott, Jennifer L. (Jennifer Lynn), author.
  Polish your poise with Madame Chic : lessons in everyday elegance / Jennifer L.
Scott.
     pages cm
  1. Charm. 2. Confidence. 3. Fashion. 4. Etiquette for women. I. Title.
  BJ1610.S3953 2015
  646.7'6—dc23
                                    2015021634

ISBN 978-1-5011-1873-9
ISBN 978-1-5011-1874-6 (ebook)

For Ben

Contents

Contents

Part 3

PRACTICING POISE

Part 1

THE POWER
OF POISE

Chapter 1

MADAME CHIC KNEW
THE POWER OF POISE

Madame Chic, my host mother as a study abroad student in Paris, looked presentable and elegant on a daily basis. It was her default way of being. When she was in the kitchen preparing breakfast in her dressing gown, she had a calm contentedness. Every day, whether at home or in the outside world, she presented herself beautifully, with flattering clothes; natural, age-appropriate makeup; and excellent grooming. She had great posture that seemed to come naturally to her. She was well-spoken and highly intelligent. She cultivated her love of cooking to an art and made our nightly dinners very elegant affairs in everything from how she set her table to how she presented the food. She had a very pleasant demeanor and was an advocate for etiquette and manners, which was evident in the way her entire family behaved. Madame Chic was a beautiful example of a poised and powerful woman.

I had never really thought much about poise before living in Paris. I was a twenty-year-old California girl who loved cutoff shorts, flip-flops, and snacking all day long. Self-discipline seemed like something boring I never wanted to have. Observing formal traditions seemed stuffy. As far as etiquette and manners went, there was just too much to remember! But all of my perceptions changed after living in Paris. Madame Chic helped me see myself in a new way. Observing what a passionate and fulfilling life she and her family led, I became open to the concept of everyday elegance. I allowed myself to believe that even this casual California girl could be graceful. I began to see that I could actually have style and learn to express myself beautifully, whether through speech or action. I learned that I too could have poise.

5 CHARACTERISTICS OF POISE

1. Confidence: Feeling comfortable in your own skin; a genuine self-assurance.
2. Composure: Keeping a positive perspective while maintaining calm self-possession.
3. Compassion: Thinking of others and practicing selflessness.
4. Presentation: Appropriately and stylishly dressed, with good posture.
5. Present: Poised people live passionately in the present moment.

Poise is defined as a graceful and elegant bearing. Madame Chic's graceful and elegant bearing certainly laid the foundation for the gracious way she lived, but it was allowing this grace and this elegance to guide every choice she made throughout the day that truly solidified her poise.

Here's the good news: *she's not the only Madame Chic in the world.* There are millions more. You've probably seen them. The woman who is stylish, self-assured, grounded, and *poised.* The woman who presents herself with grace and dignity, speaks elegantly, who lives every day as though it were a special gift. The woman with the air of mystery who cultivates her mind and seeks out the arts. The woman with the lovely home, who is not a slave to shopping. The woman who walks through her day as though she knows a delicious secret.

We are all capable of living with style, grace, and elegance. It doesn't matter what your past was like. It doesn't matter how you grew up. It doesn't matter how you behaved yesterday or even in the last hour. It doesn't matter how much money you have. It doesn't matter what the people in your family live like. It doesn't matter if your circle of friends are not interested in this subject. It doesn't matter if your family doesn't understand you. The only thing that matters is that we are all capable of change—of transformation. No one is born a Madame Chic. Dignity, grace, style, and elegance are all learned behaviors. Anyone can cultivate these attributes. It doesn't matter who you are or how hopeless your situation may seem. You can elevate your life with poise.

Poise has always been a subject of fascination in the entertainment world. Take George Bernard Shaw's *Pygmalion* or the musical adaptation, *My Fair Lady*. Take *Gigi*, *Pretty Woman*, *The Princess Diaries*, and *Sabrina*. We love a good transformation story. We love watching the caterpillar turn into the butterfly. Why do we love this story? Because deep down we believe that we are all capable of a beautiful transformation, and that gives us hope. We don't have to say, "I wish I could be like that," or "Too bad I'm just not that way." No. We can be inspired and say, "If she can do it, so can I."

There is nothing more powerful than a changed mind. The moment you change your mind and decide you'd like to pay more attention to your appearance, you ignite that power. Once you change your mind and decide you'd like to conquer shyness; when you decide to turn your smartphone off for a while; when you catch a glimpse of yourself in a store window and decide you want to stop slouching; when you decide you'd like to remain levelheaded during disagreements; when you decide you'd like to have confidence when presenting your next pitch at work; when you change your mind and decide to clean up your language—amazing things can happen.

A voice in your head will try to stop this transformation. It will make you question yourself: "Who do you think you are?" "You are a phony." "You are a fraud." "People are going to think you're pretentious." "You are going to lose your friends." "Everyone is going to think you are stuck-up." "No one is going to like you anymore."

Pay no attention to this voice. You have made up your mind to be your own version of Madame Chic. You will stand out with your grace, with your elegance, with your chicness, with your poise—for poise is a very powerful thing, indeed.

Poise is silent. It is intangible. It is under the surface. It is mysterious, but we intuitively know when someone has it. There is something attractive about that person. If you meet a poised person, her confidence and friendliness put you at ease. Being poised is not about being a robotic Stepford wife who looks perfect and acts perfect and doesn't show emotion.

Being poised is being aware of oneself and one's surroundings and being flexible and adaptable.

This is not to say that the poised person never gets flustered, or that the poised person never loses her temper. This is not to say that the poised person never steps out of line. But the poised person is self-aware. She is driven by faith, inner peace, and high standards. These are the tools she uses to get through any situation in life.

This book discusses cultivating poise rather than attaining or acquiring it. This is because poise is something that one works toward for the rest of one's life. Poise isn't something you can simply acquire like an item you buy in a shop and then never think about again. We've all heard that expression "money can't buy class." *Poise, also known as class, is not something you can acquire.* It's something you practice on a daily basis. Poise as a way of life is an art form. Just as an artist strives to perfect her art throughout her life, we will work on our poise.

Poised	Not So Poised
Has good posture	Slouches
Speaks clearly	Mumbles
Makes eye contact	Has shifty eyes
Is dressed presentably	Is sloppily dressed
Is well groomed	Needs to wash hair
Controls temper	Is quick to argue
Is well mannered	What manners?
Is a good listener	Would rather talk than listen
Has an ordered home life	Has a chaotic home life
Is kind and forgiving	Is argumentative and aggressive
Maintains an air of mystery	Shares life story on Facebook every day

Poised	Not So Poised
Accepts compliments graciously	Deflects compliments
Puts screen time in its place	Addicted to the smartphone
Uses clean language	Curses regularly
Cultivates her mind	Is done with learning
Seeks out the arts	Is content with reality TV marathons
Savors her food	Eats on the run
Takes pride in everything she does	Sees what she can get out of a situation
Savors the good times	Waits for the other shoe to drop
Keeps the faith in difficult times	Believes the worst

This is not to say that when you cultivate poise you handle every situation that comes your way with calm perfection. No. Just when you think you've mastered the art of poise, something unexpected will happen that will test you. A driver will cut you off on the road, and, overcome with rage, you might shout an obscenity and shake your fist out the window. These things happen. But the key is you will catch yourself. And because you catch yourself, you might choose a different response next time. Poise is keeping your wits about you so that when you have a negative experience, you can learn from it and handle the situation better next time.

You can cultivate poise from the moment you wake up until the moment you sleep. You can choose good posture when you're exhausted and feel like slumping over. You can pause before snapping at your spouse. You can remain firm when teaching your children common courtesy. You can take the high road when a coworker makes a snide comment. You can avoid the office lunchtime gossip session. You can have the self-respect to say no when someone is taking advantage of you. You can accept a compliment graciously. You can be a powerful role model for your children, your family, and the people in your community. You realize that you are a significant part of society and that your poise has an impact. You can do all of this and still enjoy your life, because this challenge is fun! Poise adds vitality to your life, and that is attractive.

The Scarcity of Poise

You can see that poise is scarce if you step out in public. But you might have to adjust your thinking first. Practicing poise is a forgotten art, and therefore we take its absence for granted. Is it really okay for your neighbor to ignore you as you pass each other on the sidewalk, or for a person to walk up to a store clerk and shout out a question without greeting the clerk first? What do you think when you hear people cursing loudly on their cell phones while they wait for the bus or see someone walk around in public sloppily dressed, with posture to match? Most people today have forgotten about poise. It's not their fault necessarily. They might not have had good role models or perhaps they weren't introduced to the concept. Society certainly doesn't help. The celebrities who pass as role models do little to provide inspiration.

We used to have high standards of behavior for those in entertainment, for example. During the golden age of Hollywood you would never have seen people grinding in thong underwear on stage at an awards show. Movie and television stars now strip down to their underwear or beyond for magazine spreads. Pop stars wear skimpy bathing suits and writhe and jiggle their oiled up backsides as close to the camera as possible. Can you imagine Audrey Hepburn's reaction if she saw such a thing? The scary thing is, we've gotten used to it.

And if we've gotten used to it, just think about our children, who have known nothing else. This vulgarity is the new normal. So while many people might think that this book is just a sweet little etiquette book, I urge you to take its contents seriously. Because the principles discussed in this book just might save our society from slipping into the oblivion of crassness.

While you may feel a bit hopeless right about now about the scarcity of poise in our society (especially after envisioning

Audrey Hepburn's reaction to twerking), I am here to tell you that there is hope.

⤳ The Commodity of Poise ⤳

Because poise is scarce, it is also a commodity. A commodity is described in the dictionary as "a useful and valuable thing." Poise is certainly useful. You'd be surprised by the doors that will open for you when you employ even just a little bit of poise. People will want to help you. You'll leave a good impression at job interviews. You will attract the right kind of romantic partner. You'll be treated with respect. Poise is useful.

And because it's so useful, it is also valuable. Getting the job you want or the promotion you've longed for is valuable. Attracting high-quality people into your life is valuable. Receiving help from others is valuable. These things elevate the quality of your life. When you practice cultivating poise on a daily basis, this valuable commodity will enrich your life.

That is not to say that you should cultivate poise to see

what you can get out of the deal. No, you should commit to cultivating poise because you long to make a change in your life; because you are ready to reach your full potential; because you no longer wish to go through your life looking as if you don't care about yourself, avoiding real connections with people and suffering from insecurities. You should cultivate poise because this is your one life and you are finally ready to bloom. You are ready to be present and to live fully. You are ready to adorn the amazing body you've been given, in whatever shape you're in, with clothes that express your true style. You're ready to enhance your beauty by doing something special with your hair or applying natural makeup. You're ready to stand straight as you walk down the sidewalk. You're ready to make eye contact with the next person you have a conversation with. You're ready for whatever conflict comes your way and aren't afraid of confrontation. You're ready to feel chic. You're ready for inner peace. You're ready for poise.

If all of this sounds enticing but impossible, don't worry. I felt the same way as an awkward student in the home of Madame Chic. One thing that has helped me tremendously is observing role models, whether fictional or real.

⤳ Role Models ⤳

One has to look hard to find good role models these days. Behaviors that were considered shocking in the past are now considered completely normal. It used to be that you could watch a movie or television show and be inspired by the poise and inherent elegance of the stars. Take any film with Grace

Kelly, Audrey Hepburn, or Cary Grant. Fred Astaire, Ginger Rogers, Laurence Olivier, Vivien Leigh. The characters these actors played had poise, and their poise was representative of the time. Who could forget how Grace Kelly's Margot Wendice responded when she was on trial in *Dial M for Murder*? Or how Audrey Hepburn's Holly Golightly maintained poise even throughout a case of the mean reds in *Breakfast at Tiffany's*? What about Cary Grant's Johnnie Aysgarth's elegant handling of money woes in *Suspicion*? For anyone who is not familiar with these actors or their classic films, I suggest taking a night or two each month to watch one of them. You'll be charmed by the stars' mannerisms, the way they dress and the way they react to stressful situations. Their behaviors might seem antiquated to you, but they don't have to be.

In addition to finding role models in classic films, you can also find them in today's society and entertainment. It's not so hard to spot them. People with poise shine like gems, and we become fascinated with them. The Duchess of Cambridge is a prime example. Why is the world so enamored with the future Queen of England? It is because she is a young person with poise. She is well dressed, well groomed, and well mannered when out in public. She is a young person who presents herself with dignity, yet she is still active, fun, and very modern.

Even though I mentioned you have to look hard for good role models in entertainment today, that doesn't mean they aren't there. They are there. It's just that they are not the most vocal in our society, so one has to look harder to find them. They are not the ones posting selfies of their newly enhanced lips or latest tattoo on Instagram. They are the ones quietly going about their business focusing on their art. So while one has to go to a bit more trouble to seek out these people, they do exist.

Classic actors with poise:

Audrey Hepburn
Joan Fontaine
Cary Grant
Vivien Leigh
Fred Astaire
Ginger Rogers
Grace Kelly

Jimmy Stewart

Katharine Hepburn

Laurence Olivier

Examples of modern actors with poise:

....

Andie MacDowell

Angela Lansbury

Audrey Tautou

Catherine Deneuve

Dame Helen Mirren

Dame Maggie Smith

Denzel Washington

Meryl Streep

Natalie Portman

Pierce Brosnan

Literary characters with poise:

....

Charlotte Brontë's Jane Eyre

Louisa May Alcott's March sisters from *Little*

Women (Jo does have a temper and a sharp
   tongue, but she tries to work on herself, and that
   is all one can ask for when cultivating poise)
Agatha Christie's Hercule Poirot and Jane Marple
Jane Austen's Elizabeth Bennet
Shakespeare's Beatrice from *Much Ado About
   Nothing*, Rosalind from *As You Like It*, and
   Desdemona from *Othello*
Alexander McCall Smith's Mma Ramotswe
Carolyn Keene's Nancy Drew
Ian Fleming's James Bond
Lewis Carroll's Alice
E. B. White's Charlotte from *Charlotte's Web* (I do
   realize that Charlotte is a spider, but she sure
   had class)

And what about real-life role models? The people who
don't have endless amounts of money to spend on personal
stylists and hairdressers. The people who aren't airbrushed
when you see them in pictures. The men and women you
come in contact with every day are the real deal. That is why

Madame Chic in Paris was such an inspiration to me. I could see that her poise was not an act. It was part of her personality, and I wanted to be like her. It is a wonderful thing to be able to observe someone you admire.

You might think you have no role models in your life to look up to, but I'm sure you do: your mother, an aunt, your grandmother, one of your teachers at school, a principal, your former dance teacher or music conductor, a next-door neighbor, a woman who works at the local fashion boutique. Keep your eye out for poise. It will shine like a diamond when you come across it, because it is so rare. If you feel bold, give this poised person a compliment. If not, merely observe her when she is with you. What is it about her that is so attractive? I guarantee it won't be just one thing, it will be many. She will have made many wise choices about the way she speaks, acts, dresses, and grooms herself; the way she sits, cultivates her mind, and chooses her entertainment.

∾ You Have Viewers Too ∾

No one is insignificant. No one is an accident. We are all valuable and we all have something to contribute to the world. You might think your sphere of influence is small, but even if you live in the middle of nowhere and only have your family and a few neighbors around, your poise can influence others in the most dramatic ways.

Some people say to me that the videos on my YouTube channel really impact their lives in an inspirational way. They urge me to keep up the good work for my viewership. But I have some surprising news to tell you. *You have viewers too.* Sure you might not have a YouTube channel, or a music video that's trending on social media. You might not be gracing the cover of a magazine, but *you too have viewers.* Your children view you. Your spouse views you. Your coworkers view you. Your neighbors view you. The moms at your children's school view you. Your children's teachers view you. The complete strangers you nod to as you cross the street view you. The barista working at the local coffee shop views you. The flight attendants on the airplane view you. You have viewers. And with these viewers you have the opportunity, the platform, to be a role model of grace and poise.

Sure, you probably thought about this already with regard to your family. Of course your children are looking up to you to see how you behave and how you carry yourself. But I bet you never thought you could have an impact on a total stranger. Let me ask you this: How many times in your life has a complete stranger made a powerful impression on you? Perhaps it was that woman at the airport who just looked so chic and effortless. Perhaps it was a man riding his bike down the street who was so handsomely dressed. Perhaps it was the woman in the waiting room at the doctor's office who had excellent posture. Perhaps it was the post office employee who surprised you with his kind courtesy. We become fascinated by strangers with poise, and in the same way strangers will become fascinated with you. You have viewers, whether you like it or not, whether you know these people or not. You are an important part of society. Are you acting like a member of the society you'd like to see? When you look at life like this, it's hard not to think about the way you live and how you'd like to make changes.

⌒ What About When No One's ⌒ Watching?

Often people who start the journey to cultivate poise only make an effort when they are in the presence of other people. While this might work temporarily, it won't feel authentic because you will be doing it for the wrong reasons. You'll feel like a fake and you may impress others that way too. *That's why how you live when no one is watching is even more important.* How can this be?

When you are alone and no one is watching, you are your true self, your most authentic. That's why it's the best time to cultivate poise and make changes in your life. If you decide to wear presentable pajamas to bed or not to gorge on an entire bag of potato chips while watching a sitcom marathon on television, you are setting the precedent for how you will behave when you are around other people. When you choose to savor your lunch at a set table rather than eating out of the microwave tray while scrolling through your texts, you are setting a precedent. When you decide to comb your hair and put on a nice dress, even when you have no plans to leave the house, you are setting a precedent for how you will present yourself in public. You are shifting the thermostat of your behavior and setting up new routines that will soon become a natural part of your life. You will then have replaced your old behaviors with new ones.

We should not cultivate poise in order to impress other people. There is no point in this pretense if you are not going to make solid changes in the way you live, whether people are watching or not. How you behave and live when you are alone is the indicator of how you live your entire life.

Now that we've explored the power of poise, let's get started on implementing it in our own lives. Let's dive right in. Cultivating poise is an adventure. Are you ready for the challenge?

Part 2

PRESENTATION

Chapter 2

THE EMPOWERMENT

OF STYLE

When I arrived in Paris fresh off the airplane from Los Angeles, I was astonished by the beauty of the city. The architecture was like nothing I had ever seen before. Not only the buildings, but the fountains and the bridges—heck, even the lampposts were beautiful! Everything about the city seemed to be well dressed, from the shop windows to the tables on the sidewalk cafés. And I haven't even gotten to the people yet! Clearly this was not a casual city. Both men and women went about their business handsomely dressed. Their clothes fit beautifully. I saw artistically wrapped scarves! Well-shod feet! Clothes that looked as if they were tailor-made for their wearer! They all presented themselves beautifully, from the vendors at the farmer's market to the executives walking into their offices. None of them looked as though they had rolled out of bed and couldn't care less how they looked. Each Parisian told this wide-eyed American how he or she wished to be perceived.

The stylistic revelations continued when I met Madame and Monsieur Chic for the first time. It was a Wednesday afternoon, and as I sat in their living room getting to know them better over a cup of tea, I noticed how smartly they were dressed: Madame Chic in her silk blouse, A-line skirt, pearls, and low heels, and Monsieur Chic in his dress pants, button-down shirt, sweater, and shiny shoes. I thought it awfully kind that they had decided to dress up to meet me. What an effort! My initial smugness over their stylistic pomp and ceremony just for me was swiftly quashed the next day when I saw that they dressed that way on a daily basis. Monsieur and Madame Chic were chic dressers, as are many Parisians. Their poise began with the way they presented themselves.

We will begin cultivating poise by focusing on style and beauty. We begin here because looking good is a great motivator! When you get your hair done at the salon or wear a new lipstick shade, it puts a spring in your step. When you wear a dress you haven't worn in a while and you receive a compliment, or when you have been taking care of your skin and it shows, you feel good about yourself. These feelings can inspire us to beautify other areas of our lives.

How you look on the outside is a direct reflection of what's going on inside. If you have worn track pants and a drab baggy T-shirt every day for the past three years, for example, you aren't celebrating the beautiful person you are and the beautiful body you've been given. Instead, you are asking the world not to look at you, telling the world that it is not worth the effort to look beyond your fashion statement.

Here's the thing: the poise does not come from a dress or a shade of lipstick, it emerges when you decide to care about the way you look. Beauty emerges from the decision to cultivate poise in the way we style ourselves. It has nothing to do with what clothes you own, having the latest makeup palette, or the expensive highlights you got at the salon last week. Beauty emerges from the self-confidence you emit and the newfound joy you take in celebrating your unique beauty.

For example, you admire a woman in a bright, beautiful dress. You wish you could wear something like that but tell yourself you could never pull it off. You think you're too fat. You think you're too shy—you wouldn't want to draw all that attention to yourself. You've never dressed like that before, so why start now? It's too late. Listen to what you are telling yourself. What if a good friend told you she had these thoughts? If you long to dress differently, to get a certain haircut or to wear that shade of lipstick, take the plunge and try it! You might feel uncomfortable initially, but once you get over your self-consciousness, real beauty blossoms.

The fun part of all of this is that we are not all the same. We all have a different sense of style. We do our hair a certain way. We all know what kind of makeup we like to wear and what looks we don't like. There is no one way to dress, or to make yourself attractive. You might have a bohemian free-spirit style. You might enjoy appearing eccentric and whimsical, or you might like an elegant, classic look. You might love vintage ladylike dresses, or you might love wearing only pants and blouses. On your journey to cultivate poise, you will become a connoisseur of your own look.

⤿ Don't Put It Off ⤾

Whatever negative feelings you have about the way you look will have to be addressed—not brushed off or dismissed, but *addressed*, so that you can move forward and celebrate the unique beauty you have been given.

As discussed above, many women say, "When I lose weight, I'll start dressing nicely." They say it for years and years, still waiting to get to that ideal weight and finally celebrate themselves. Let me tell you something, if you lose the weight you'd like to lose, congratulations! If you don't, you are still a significant human being. Your weight, the number on the scale, does not define you and should not prevent you from dressing and adorning yourself beautifully. I have a theory that once you start to dress well every day, you will most likely be inspired to lose the weight and actually have a better shot at it. This is because you are not approaching your weight loss with a defeatist mentality.

If you are in the midst of a weight-loss process and are uncertain of which size to buy, keep in mind that you can get your clothing tailored. If you have a beloved dress but it's now too big because you've lost weight, a skilled tailor can make it fit again. It will probably look even better after a tailor has worked on it because it will be custom formed to fit your body.

Je Suis la Femme

So many readers have written to me about the Madame Chic books saying, "Jennifer, I used to dress like a man every day, and now I am embracing my femininity and am loving it!" Embracing one's femininity is not easy to do, especially if you are not used to doing this or if you have no feminine role models in your life. Once you start to embrace your femininity, you will undoubtedly get a lot of attention from other people: "You look fancy!" or "Ooh where are you going?" or "Someone looks nice today!" You might feel overdressed or self-conscious about this. You might feel annoyed by the compliments you are receiving. As someone who shies away from attention, I completely understand this. Just graciously accept every compliment you receive. When they ask you where you're going, tell them, and when they say "Wow, you're just wearing that to pick up your child from school?" say yes with a smile and move on. Remember you have viewers. You are a role model and perhaps the fact that you dress well will inspire others who secretly wish to do the same. It's important that to make others feel more comfortable we don't waiver on our mission. If you are ready to make this radical change in your life, you will make waves, and that might not be in your comfort zone. But push through, *mon ami*. You can do it. And I promise you, you will make a great difference in your sphere of influence.

Casual Clothes

The exercise clothes trap

It makes me sad to see a beautiful woman (and I believe all women are beautiful!) wearing frumpy workout clothes day in and day out as her regular attire. How can one blossom that way? It's one thing if you're actually exercising, then of course, wear your exercise clothes. And many people have to run errands after exercising, or drop their kids off at school before exercising. This has happened to me on many an occasion, so I understand the need to wear your exercise clothes to places other than the gym. However, there are many who wear their exercise clothes all day every day. If this is ringing true for you, it could be time to analyze why you wear your exercise clothes all day long. Is it because they are comfortable? Is it so you don't have to think about putting an outfit together? Is it because it's just what you've always done and you're afraid to make a change? Is it merely a matter of convenience?

I have seen some very chic exercise clothes out there. Just walk down Montana Avenue in Santa Monica, where I live, and you will see many examples. But I still believe, no matter how chic the exercise clothes, there is a time and a place for them.

Loungewear

Loungewear is a nice term for ratty clothes we wear at home. I don't believe in loungewear. This is because I believe that people should wear their outside clothes inside. I advocate looking presentable always, not just when you are at work or out running errands where people can see you, but also behind closed doors. Many people look presentable when out in public and then, the minute they get home, change into sweatpants or some worn-out old outfit that isn't fit to see the light of day.

Madame Chic did not wear loungewear. When she dressed for the day, that was it. She would normally wear an A-line skirt, a sweater or blouse, stockings, flats or low-heeled shoes, and always her pearls. If she went outside, she usually wore her coat or a cardigan, a scarf, and gloves. When she came home from running errands, she remained in her day clothes. She never wandered around the house in her sweatpants (of course she didn't own sweatpants at all!). She never changed into her pajamas early.

People often ask me: "Jennifer, I love your outfits, but what do you wear when you come home for the day?" I wear what you see in my ten-item wardrobe! Yes, I will wear a dress and stockings at home. Yes, I will wear a pair of black trousers and a blouse with a nice necklace at home. You will find me in the kitchen every evening cooking dinner in my day clothes. I will simply put an apron on. You will find me cleaning the house in my day clothes, again with an apron on. The only time I will change to other clothes is if I'm doing gardening, but sometimes I don't even change for that! You will often see me in the yard wearing (you guessed it) an apron over my nice clothes along with gloves.

Why do I advocate this? Because we are not cultivating poise to show off for other people. We are doing it to change our lives. Our entire lives. Not just our public lives, but our private lives too. You feel and act differently when you are wearing nice clothes rather than frumpy sweatpants and an oversized T-shirt. I don't care if you live alone and no one is going to see you all day. It is about self-respect.

It is so important for us to remain presentable when we are at home, especially when we have children. Most of their memories of you will be at home. As was previously mentioned, you don't want your children to look back on you and only remember you in yoga pants! Dare to be stylish at home.

Another question I am asked a lot is: "What happens if I stain my nice clothes?" Of course we don't want to ruin our nice, high-quality clothes. Let me tell you from experience, the likelihood that you will ruin a garment is extremely slim. I have two toddlers who love to paint, love to dig in the dirt, and generally love to make grandiose messes, and in my now five-plus years of raising them, I have only ever ruined one item of clothing: a T-shirt that got nail polish on it. I painted my daughter's nails with children's polish, and she instantly gave me a hug and wiped her nails all over my shirt. Oh well! I would have traded a thousand shirts for that hug; it wasn't a big deal. (If I had been wearing an apron, by the way, the shirt wouldn't have been ruined. Now you know to wear an apron if you're painting your daughter's nails!) Most of the time, when you get a stain on your clothes, you can get it out.

Some people have special circumstances and will want to change when they get home. I understand that. Let's say you wear a suit to work and would like to change when you get home. Then it is a good idea to have presentable clothes to wear at home: leggings, a tunic sweater, and ballet flats, for example. Please promise to banish all old, tattered, stained, oversized, over-worn clothes from your closet. The minute one of your garments shows wear and tear, if you can't mend it, then get rid of it. Madame Chic taught me to always use the best things you have. I always feel better when I have taken the time to present myself well, no matter what is on my schedule for the day. Try wearing your day clothes at home. Push through the urge to change your clothes when you get home. Soon, looking presentable will come easily to you, like second nature.

⁓ True Style ⁓

What is your true style? Is it represented by the clothes that you currently have? I am always surprised when people have no idea what their true style is. It should be obvious to you. It's how you would dress if nothing else mattered. If your style isn't apparent to you, it's because your stylistic eye is being clouded by outside influences—trends, celebrities, popular culture, your friends, or your community. It's time to forget all of those influences for a moment. If you could dress however you wanted, what would you wear?

If you feel as though you are dressing in a way that isn't "you," ask yourself if your community is affecting the way you dress. Let's say, for example, most of the women your age dress in short shorts and crop tops, but you favor a more refined style. Break away from the pack and wear that pretty floral dress with the soft cardigan and sandals. Yes, you will stand out, but if you are going to cultivate poise, you are going to stand out anyway, so you might as well do it in style!

Madame Chic was certainly not interested in trends. Her style was classic, modest, and traditional. A-line skirts, high-quality sweaters, silk blouses, low-heeled shoes, and classic accessories were the adornments that made her feel comfortable. People who embrace their true style look comfortable and in turn make other people comfortable in their presence. As you use the ten-item wardrobe on a daily basis, your true style will come into focus more than ever. Keep this in mind when shopping for new items for your capsule wardrobe. Make sure that you don't make a purchase that doesn't fall in line with your true style. This discipline is very helpful when you are tempted to make a purchase just because something is on sale. If it's not your true style and doesn't fit in with the ten-item wardrobe you've cultivated, it has no place in your closet. Save your money and be patient. When you find that perfect dress for your chosen wardrobe, you will be so happy you had the self-discipline to wait for it.

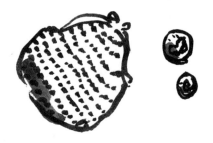

Quiz: Know Your True Style

If you suffer from true style confusion, it is helpful to look at the sorts of things you enjoy in life to home in on how to stylistically express yourself. Take this quiz and find out if you are in line with your true style. Write down the number from your favorite option in each category then find your results at the end of the quiz.

This film gets you every time:

1. *Amélie*
2. *Breakfast at Tiffany's*
3. *The Notebook*
4. *Stand by Me*
5. *Almost Famous*
6. *Dead Poet's Society*
7. *Clueless*

Your favorite flowers are:

1. Tulips
2. Orchids
3. English roses
4. Gerbera daisies
5. Wildflowers
6. Hydrangeas
7. Bird-of-paradise

You just adore this actress:

1. Marion Cotillard
2. Angelina Jolie
3. Keira Knightley
4. Katharine Hepburn
5. Kate Hudson
6. Reese Witherspoon
7. Sarah Jessica Parker

Your inspirational style icon is:

1. Inès de la Fressange
2. Jacqueline Kennedy Onassis
3. Grace Kelly
4. Diane Keaton
5. Drew Barrymore
6. Gwyneth Paltrow
7. Nicole Richie

If you could wear only one fashion brand it would be:

1. Chanel
2. Diane von Furstenberg
3. Vera Wang
4. Vince
5. Free People
6. Ralph Lauren
7. Alexander McQueen

Your favorite play or musical is:

1. *Gigi*
2. *Chicago*
3. *Romeo and Juliet*
4. *West Side Story*
5. *A Midsummer Night's Dream*
6. *Barefoot in the Park*
7. *Waiting for Godot*

Your favorite book is:

1. *A Moveable Feast*
2. *The Great Gatsby*
3. *Jane Eyre*
4. *Huckleberry Finn*
5. *On the Road*
6. *The Catcher in the Rye*
7. *Confessions of a Shopaholic*

This leading man makes your heart beat faster:

1. Owen Wilson in *Midnight in Paris*
2. Cary Grant in anything
3. Colin Firth as Mr. Darcy in *Pride and Prejudice*
4. Harrison Ford as Indiana Jones
5. Johnny Depp in *Pirates of the Caribbean*
6. Matt Damon in *Good Will Hunting*
7. Richard Gere in *Pretty Woman*

If you could time travel to any period, you would go to:

1. Paris right now!
2. Hollywood in its golden age
3. Jane Austen's England
4. The Wild West
5. Woodstock in the sixties
6. The Hamptons circa 1985
7. Andy Warhol's Factory in New York City

Mostly 1s: Parisian Chic—You love fashion and aren't afraid to experiment with an eclectic, fashionable look. You feel equally comfortable in a beautiful form-fitting dress with heels or in jeans, Converse, and a Chanel jacket. You are totally comfortable in your own style and answer to no trend.

Mostly 2s: Sophisticated Glamour—Looking polished is important to you. You love bold accessories and cocktail dresses. When dressing down, you keep it chic by accenting your casual look with high-end accessories. Always well groomed, your style is timeless and sophisticated.

Mostly 3s: Romantic Feminine—You feel most comfortable wearing dresses with feminine accents. Silks and cashmere are your favorite fabrics. You love floral prints and traditional, vintage looks. Always tasteful, you prefer ladylike hems and necklines but still know how to look alluring.

Mostly 4s: Low-Maintenance Chic—A tomboy at heart, you prefer trousers and shorts over dresses and skirts for everyday wear. Simple clothes without fussy adornments are your preference. You are athletic and outdoorsy and often find yourself active throughout the day, and your clothing reflects this. At night you love wearing a tuxedo trouser with a great silk tank top, or a simple yet striking dress, and have been known on occasion to wear red lipstick.

Mostly 5s: Bohemian—You are a free spirit and your fashion choices reflect this. Artistic in nature, you love maxi skirts, cowboy boots, eclectic jewelry, and a good fringe. You embrace your natural hair, whether you have curly locks or long, straight tresses.

Mostly 6s: Preppy—Nothing feels more comfortable than your crisp polo shirt, the perfect jeans, and a great pair of suede loafers. You keep your evening wear simple yet elegant. Fresh, natural makeup, understated jewelry, and a simple hairstyle let your natural beauty radiate.

Mostly 7s: Fashion Forward—You don't follow the trends, you set them. Lover of the avant-garde and not shy *du tout*, you have no qualms about experimenting with everything from your haircut to your manicure. Fashion-wise, statement shoulders, statement jewelry, and the latest high-heel design are what excite you most. You can be a chameleon and have no fear experimenting with fashion.

Chapter 3

PRESENTABLE CLOTHES

How do our clothes relate to our poise? Why does what we wear matter so much? Every day we stand in front of our wardrobes and make a choice of how we will clothe ourselves. This might seem like an insignificant thing—just another choice to make in a long list of choices—but how we dress ourselves matters deeply. The right clothing can help you thrive. Standing in front of your closet every morning should be a joy, not a chore. You should get excited about what to wear every day. This excitement will prompt you to want to dress your best on a daily basis. Poised people always strive to be presentably and appropriately dressed for every occasion. They know that expressing their style through their clothing is their visual calling card to the world.

⌒ Poise and the Ten-Item Wardrobe ⌒

The ten-item wardrobe is arguably the most popular topic I write about. Women are intrigued by it, primarily because most of us have so many clothes, we can't even fathom how we would live with less. In fact having an extensive wardrobe (in many cases, hundreds of garments) is a relatively new phenomenon; our grandmothers and great-grandmothers got along just fine with much less (and very stylishly I might add). What do our overstuffed closets have to do with poise? Our closets full of clothes that we never wear tell us we are confused, that we have little self-control, that we have an issue with needing new things all the time, that we are lazy and don't want to go through our clothes and donate the ones we don't need. Not to be a total downer, but our overstuffed closets are filled not only with clothes but also with unresolved issues.

Your closet is a great place to start if you want to develop poise and work on your inner chic. If you haven't already done so, I highly recommend that you try out the ten-item wardrobe. The ten-item-wardrobe journey will reveal so much to you and bring up issues you never even knew you had—issues ranging from style and spending habits to self-worth. The ten-item wardrobe is discussed in both *Lessons from Madame Chic* and *At Home with Madame Chic*, but it is helpful to review its basic concepts here.

Clear the wardrobe clutter

If you have too many clothes, you will be confused and distracted each morning when choosing an outfit. I'm going to help you clear out all of the clutter in your wardrobe. Assess all of your clothes. Your instinct will tell you what needs to go. But if you need a rule, here it is: get rid of everything you haven't worn in a year. Ignore the not-so-poised voice that tells you that the unused clothes are your style, or that you might wear them one day. You know deep down that's not true. Get radical here. Donate the clothes. Get rid of them. You don't need them; someone else does. Once you donate all of the clothes that you haven't worn in a year, that don't fit you, that aren't your true style, and that just simply don't belong, organize the clothes you have left. Store everything that is not suitable for the season you are currently in. If it's the middle of summer, you don't need to open your closet and see your winter parka every morning.

Past its prime?

If you still need convincing to get rid of garments that are past their prime, perhaps this story will motivate you. One Sunday I was running late for church. I had about ten minutes to get dressed. It was cold and rainy outside, so I wanted to wear opaque tights with my dress and rain boots. I keep all of my stockings and tights in the same compartment in my lingerie drawer. I started looking for my opaque tights. Then I remembered that both of my two good pairs were hanging up to dry, because I had washed them the night before. I knew there was a third one in there, so I started digging in my drawer. My digging became more frantic and furious as I sifted through all of my stockings, which, at this point, all looked the same. I finally came across the pair I was looking for, put them on, and headed out the door with my family. As we began to walk to church, I realized with horror that my tights didn't have any elastic in the waist and were slowly sinking down toward my feet. "Mommy, what's wrong?" my daughter asked as I started to seriously fidget to correct the wardrobe malfunction.

When we got to church, I went straight to the bathroom to see if I could fix the problem. Without any safety pins or tape my efforts were pointless. I briefly considered taking the tights off altogether, but it was so cold outside and I didn't want to freeze. I decided that I could get through the service with minimal movement and that everything would be okay. And it was, until we stood up to receive communion. As I made my way in the procession to the head of the church, my stockings started to fall. *Rapidly.* So much so that the crotch of the tights was at my knees by the time I shimmied up to the pastor! What's the moral of this story? If an article of clothing is worn out and past its prime, *you must get rid of it.* Why I didn't throw those tights away after the elastic wore out I will never know, but I tell you, I'll never make that mistake again!

The poised choice

Now it's time to fall in love again with all of the clothes that made the cut. Perhaps many of them are nice and you have avoided wearing them so as not to "ruin" them. You need to put aside the idea that you must save your best clothes for later. I'm not talking about wearing a lace cocktail dress to the grocery store, but I am talking about wearing that nice silk blouse that you never use. Get into the habit of wearing your nice clothes on a regular basis. Poised people always put thought into their presentation. They do not settle for drab, old clothes because they're saving their best for a later day. Each day is a gift. Each day could be your last day on earth! Don't save your nice clothes for later, wear them *today*.

When you choose your outfit each morning, ask yourself what the poised choice would be. When you are choosing between wearing jeans and a T-shirt (again) and a nice dress, you might feel inspired to pick the dress. There is definitely a time and a place for jeans and T-shirts, but if you find that you wear them exclusively, see if you can change it up and make a choice that isn't initially in your comfort zone. Soon, your comfort zone will shift, and jeans and a T-shirt might begin to feel too casual and un-special for you. The dress will now be in your comfort zone. As we make the poised choice each day, we shift our perception of chic in the right direction.

∾ Ten Core Pieces ∾

The "ten" in the ten-item wardrobe refers to the ten (or insert number here that works for you) core pieces. These are the foundation pieces that you wear every day, that you build your looks from. Pants (including jeans), dresses, blouses, and skirts are all core pieces. These are the ones you will really have to think about. Ideally, many of them will be high-quality pieces that will last you more than one season. They will be pieces that you love and feel comfortable in. They will be in colors that flatter you and are easy to mix and match. As you move forward, you will make the poised choice with these wardrobe staples. As the seasons go on, you will learn from the past choices you have made—mistakes and all. You won't purchase a dress if it looks as if it's already too short and might shrink. You won't purchase those pants that look as if they might become too tight after a few washes. You'll find your favorite jeans brand and the style that looks best on you. You'll realize the climate you live in is too consistently hot for long-sleeved blouses. You might find that layering is in your best interest. You might discover a particular style of dress that is very flattering for your shape. You will create a collection of clothes that fit you beautifully, that flatter you and complement you. These clothes will represent your true style. The only way to reach this clarity is by getting serious about your ten-item wardrobe.

Sample core items:

4 dresses
2 pairs of trousers
4 blouses

or

2 pairs of jeans
2 pairs of trousers
4 blouses
2 dresses

or

3 dresses
2 skirts
3 blouses
2 pairs of jeans

or

10 dresses

Now, how crucial is the number ten? Not crucial at all. If you cannot fathom having only ten core items, you can have fifteen or twenty or even twenty-five. The point is to develop a discerning eye about your core items first. You might find over time that you don't need so many items and that ten is a number that actually works really well for you. I have many readers who successfully adhere to the ten core items. I also have many who have fifteen or twenty and write to me saying their new approach to their wardrobes has transformed their lives. This is powerful stuff!

The ten-item wardrobe also gives you a foundation and a structure for clothes shopping. It encourages discernment and self-discipline in spending. It champions quality over quantity and will test your creativity by requiring you to appreciate the clothes you already have and find new ways of wearing them. It is a slow burn, but a very satisfactory one. You can apply the ten-item wardrobe tenants to how you shop for everything, not just clothes. You will only shop when necessary. When you do need to purchase something, you'll have a strong idea of what it is you need and not settle for anything less. You can still partake in sale shopping, but only if what you are looking for is an item of need that will be used, useful, beautiful, and/or loved. Whatever you do buy fits in gloriously with the integrity of your home and other belongings.

You are no longer just stuffing items into your closet without analyzing what first needs to go. You will slow down enough to give yourself the needed space by getting rid of clothes that are past their prime and no longer suit you.

When cultivating poise in your clothes shopping, before making any purchase, ask yourself the following questions:

....

Do I truly need this?
Can I afford this?
What are the reasons I'm buying this?
Do I want this?
Will I still want this next week or even next year?

The benefits of the ten-item wardrobe are vast. Your shopping habits will become healthier. You will waste less money; you will not be a slave to consumerism; you won't be tempted by the old pulls that used to draw you in (*Final sale! Clearance! Last chance!*). You will clarify your true style and embrace it. You will be forced to wear your nice clothes on a daily basis by getting rid of the ragged or unflattering ones, and therefore you will look presentable always. When you wake up in the morning, the choice of what to wear will be easy because everything in your wardrobe will go with everything else. Poised people look presentable, assert their style, and are comfortable in their clothing. The ten-item wardrobe will get you there. Don't be shy, just try it!

Effortless outfit planning

When you have taken all of the necessary steps to implement the ten-item wardrobe, you will be amazed at how easy it is to put an outfit together. Having only a handful of outfits eliminates the confusion of too many choices. The outfits you have thought out beforehand will express your true style. Skeptics of the ten-item wardrobe worry they will get bored with their clothes. This is not an issue because the possibilities are many, and you will have so much fun making combinations from what you have. Also, if you get bored, you have a marvelous opportunity for personal growth in learning to be satisfied with what you already have. This builds character, and all of these personal triumphs will aid in the cultivation of poise.

A dress is the easiest choice because all you have to think about is the accessories that go with it: stockings, shoes, jewelry, and outerwear. This is why dresses are always well represented in my ten-item wardrobe. Tops and bottoms should be easy to combine; if you plan your wardrobe carefully, you won't need to agonize over an outfit to see if it "goes." After years of practice, you will be so confident in your true style that everything in your wardrobe will live in harmony with everything else, making outfit planning effortless.

Extras

Extras are all of the items in your wardrobe that help your outfits come together: T-shirts, layering pieces such as sweaters and cardigans, outerwear, accessories such as scarves and jewelry, handbags, and shoes. Use your extras to custom tailor your ten-item wardrobe to your particular lifestyle. If you live in a cold climate, you will need more sweaters than someone living in Southern California. If you have young children and find yourself at the park often, you might need more T-shirts. If you walk a lot, you will need more flat shoes. The key with the extras is to keep the capsule-wardrobe mentality while selecting them. You don't want to get smug with your ten core items and go bananas with hundreds of extras. That doesn't count! And while there is no right number for how many extras are perfect for you, you will know where to add and subtract in this area. Extras are almost more compelling than the core pieces because you can get creative here. It's the extras that allow your core items to achieve so many varied looks. It's amazing what a statement necklace or a pretty scarf can do to an outfit. Be just as discerning with your extras as you are with your core items and remember to relax and have fun with them.

Accessories, glorious accessories

If you still feel intimidated by the process of putting an outfit together, start by wearing simple basics, such as a blue jersey dress or a green V-necked sweater with jeans, and plan on embellishing your look with accessories such as scarves and/ or jewelry (more on this in a moment). When you shop, keep on the lookout for simple, non-patterned clothes that fit you well. These clothes can act as a blank canvas for styling. Contrary to what you might think, you will not get bored easily with these simple basics, because there are so many ways to accessorize them.

For example, let's say you have a blue cotton jersey dress. It has a crew neck and cap sleeves and is a flattering length that is comfortable for you. Today you might pair it with your yellow scarf and tan espadrilles. Later in the week, you might wear it with your red ballet flats and gold bib necklace. On date night you might wear it with nude heels and a lightweight patterned cardigan. You see, the possibilities are endless, and because it is such a "neutral" dress, you can't go wrong.

Shoes

Shoes see everything; there are no
secrets we can keep from our shoes.
—Alexander McCall Smith,
The Double Comfort Safari Club

You are either a shoe person or you are not. If you are not, may I suggest you become one? This does not mean you need to channel Carrie Bradshaw and go bankrupt buying Manolo

Blahniks, but this does mean that you start to care about what you put on your feet. Choose to purchase quality over quantity. Clean, presentable shoes are so important. I have found after many years of experience, and after being married to a husband who works in the shoe industry and visiting factories all over Europe, that high-quality shoes are the best way to go. It is so much better to have a few pairs of high-quality shoes that look great, feel comfortable, and last a long time, than it is to have dozens, if not hundreds, of lesser quality shoes filling your closet shelves.

The first high-quality pair of heels I ever bought were from Ferragamo. I was in my mid-twenties and decided I didn't want to wear cheap shoes that fell apart and looked tattered after only a few wears. Ferragamo has a sale once a year, so I waited for it and drove my little car to Beverly Hills to check it out. When I walked into the store, I felt very intimidated. Everything was so nice. So expensive! I didn't quite feel as if I belonged. I was more used to stores like Payless ShoeSource. But the sales associate was very kind and attentive, and I tried on a pair of low-heeled tan suede pumps. They were the sort of shoes that would never go out of style and I knew that. I could wear them for business or an evening out. They were exceptionally comfortable as I walked around the carpeted floor. They were also 40 percent off the retail price. I was sold.

As I write this eight and a half years later, I still have this pair of shoes. I still wear them on a regular basis. I've had them resoled once and they have never given me grief. I take good care of them by keeping them protected in a shoe bag and trying not to get them wet. The couple hundred dollars I spent on those shoes have certainly been worth it. Over the years they have more than paid for themselves, and if I hadn't bought them but had settled for many more less expensive pairs, I would have wasted money in the long run.

Classic shoes to invest in:
....

Black pumps (suede, leather, and/or patent leather)

*Tan or beige pumps (suede, leather,
and/or patent leather)*

*Low-heeled pumps (for more conservative
occasions or when you will have to be on your
feet all day; most of my heels are low heels)*

*Black leather boots (heel height
depends on your preference)*

Brown leather boots

Ballet flats

*Driving loafers (wonderfully comfortable
and so presentable looking)*

*Rain boots (you might be able to get a great deal
on these after rainy season is over with)*

*Fancy event shoes (pick something neutral, such as silver
or gold, that will go with many an evening choice)*

Strappy sandals with a heel (for summer evenings)

A WORD ON SANDALS

Living in Southern California makes me somewhat
of a connoisseur of flat sandals. I know to purchase
one or two per year and that they most likely will not
last me longer than the season, as I take them to the
beach, to the park, and beyond. I know that many
high-quality, expensive options are available for me
here, but I choose to buy mid-range sandals that will
be comfortable but will also have a shorter shelf life
than the other shoes I purchase. Seek out what works
best for you, and just remember to keep them as clean

and presentable as possible. If you are wearing an open-toed shoe, make sure your feet are groomed and pleasant to look at.

You are most likely not going to be able to purchase all of these in one go. You might find that you can only buy one or two pairs of shoes this year. That's okay. Employ self-discipline here and don't be tempted to purchase them all with your credit card. If you can only purchase one or two this year then get the most versatile, classic shoes first. Purchase that low-heeled black suede pump that you can wear to a work presentation, the theater and out to a nice dinner. It is easier to make the classic shoes work with your wardrobe.

When your shoes start displaying signs of wear and tear, you must either have them fixed, or if they are beyond repair, you must get rid of them. Wearing tatty shoes can ruin an outfit and the impression you are trying to make. Vogue editor Diana Vreeland famously polished the soles of her shoes and once said, "unshined shoes are the *end* of civilization."

Madame Chic wore classic, high-quality shoes and only

had a few pairs. She never wore high heels but preferred a low-heeled pump. For everyday wear, she wore high-quality leather flats, usually with a buckle. According to the *Daily Mail*, Queen Elizabeth II of England has worn the same style of shoe for fifty years. The shoes, handmade by Anello & Davide of Kensington, are high-quality and pricey, but the Queen gets her money's worth by re-heeling them when they wear out. Queen Elizabeth is clearly not concerned about keeping up with the trends or reinventing the wheel when it comes to stylish shoes. She has found a comfortable, high-quality, stylish shoe, and she has stuck with it. Catherine, the Duchess of Cambridge, often does the same thing. There have been numerous articles written about how the Duchess favors the L.K. Bennett nude patent sledge shoe (which has a terrible name but is quite a nice-looking shoe). The Duchess is practical and knows that this neutral shoe will complement many an outfit. Classic design is timeless.

Scarves

When you add a scarf to your outfit, you can't help but feel a little more poised. Before I went to live in Paris with Madame

Chic, the only scarf I owned was a giant fleece number I'd wear to early morning band practice. Upon arriving in Paris, I immediately noticed how French women artistically draped their scarves around their necks, not only providing protection from the cold, but also individualizing their outfit in a stylish way.

If you live in a cold climate, to keep you warm you will need a small collection of scarves that you rotate. If you don't live in a cold climate, you can use scarves as stylish accessories. The great thing is that you don't need to own too many scarves, you just need to know how to tie them.

WAYS TO TIE A SCARF

Le Simple: Hold both ends of the scarf together and drape it around your neck, the ends on one side and the U-shaped fold on the other. Thread the ends of the scarf through the U-shaped fold. Pull until the loop is near your neck. *C'est simple!*

Le Parisian: Unfold the scarf, bunch it in a rectangle, and hold it evenly in front of your neck. Wrap one side around your neck clockwise, and the other counterclockwise. Tie the ends once and, if needed, twice. Fluff the scarf until it sits how you like it on your neck.

Le Gypsy: Fold your scarf into a large triangle. Keeping the point of the triangle toward your feet, bring the two ends around your neck until they once again meet in front, and tie them into a knot either on top of the scarf or beneath it to create this bohemian "bib" look.

L'artiste: Look as if you just stepped out of the art studio by taking a voluminous scarf and wrapping one side clockwise and the other counterclockwise around your neck, tucking the ends into the folds around your neck to conceal them. This gives the illusion of a longer neck and emits an air of insouciance.

Le Lady: Fold the scarf into a triangle. Wrap your scarf around your shoulders as if it were a shawl. Take the two ends and tie them into a knot and then into a knot again, allowing the scarf to cover your shoulders beautifully. I often wear this look with jeans and a T-shirt to "class up" my casual look.

L'infinity: If you don't own an infinity scarf, you can create one by tying the ends of your scarf into a tiny knot at the very end, creating a giant circle. Wrap the scarf around your head twice and conceal the knotted end.

Le Twist: Holding out your scarf lengthwise, twist it by turning your hands in opposing directions until it doubles up on itself. Then, as with *Le Simple* above, fold the scarf in half, with the ends on one side and the loop on the other. Drape it around your neck and thread the ends through the loop.

Le Butterfly: Tie your scarf in one knot below the front of your neck. Take the outward portion of each long strand hanging down and tie them together in a small knot behind your neck (in the back). This creates the effect of butterfly wings. Now, tuck under the remaining lowest point of the scarf until it sits how you like it.

THE POISED PURSE

It's a good idea to clean out your purse at least once a week. When it gets too heavy, it starts to affect your posture. During the week, I tend to collect a large assortment of items in my handbag: wet wipes, a pair of girls' socks, an e-reader, old receipts, loose change, three types of lip gloss, headphones. Oh yeah, it's all in there. Right along with crumbs, twigs (don't ask), and pens that have lost their caps. If you clean out your handbag, you won't be frantically shuffling through it to find your ringing cell phone (not so chic). The essentials to always have on hand are keys, wallet, phone, change in a change purse, breath mints, tissues, compact with mirror, lip gloss, and hand sanitizer.

Jewelry

Coco Chanel famously suggested that you take off one accessory before leaving the house so you do not look overdone. Jewelry is a creative way to add punctuation to any outfit. You might be the type to only wear your diamond stud earrings and a simple necklace, or you might be more daring and try out the many statement pieces available today. Whether you appreciate a bold use of jewelry or prefer more understated adornments, make sure you are not wearing too much. Keep Ms. Chanel's sage advice in mind before leaving the house. Have fun using jewelry to enhance your outfit, and remember not to go overboard with it.

⌇ Sleepwear ⌇

You know what I'm going to say. Let's all say it together: "Your sleepwear should be presentable!" There are so many options for presentable pajamas: chemises, nightgowns, sleep shirts, button-down pajamas, legging sets, and more. You can express your true style here as well. I love doing this! I like to keep it elegant and sophisticated, even at bedtime, so you probably won't see me in a reindeer onesie. I like to wear slip-like nightgowns in the summer and button-down pajamas in the winter. I always wear them with a dressing gown or robe if I'm outside of bed (more on this in the next section). I tend to buy nice, quality nightgowns that last a long time. I might only purchase a new nightie once a year. I wash them on delicate and hang-dry them if needed. My style might not be your style. You might love a flirty teddy or a hot-pink button-down pajama with the Eiffel Tower on it. Whatever your style is: express it at bedtime!

Why are presentable pajamas important? Because we want to be our best, poised selves at all times of the day *and night*. Yes, even when we're sleeping! We are growing out of the sloppiness of our teenage and college years, when we wore boxer shorts and oversized concert T-shirts to bed. While your pajamas can still be playful, they can also reflect the self-respect and dignity that you deserve. Presentable pajamas are another component in presenting yourself well. They indicate that you are cultivating poise for the right reasons: not to impress other people, but to see the change it makes in your own life.

The dressing gown

Lord Grantham: I nearly came down
in a dinner jacket tonight.
The Dowager Countess: Oh really?
Well, why not a dressing gown? Or
better still pajamas?

—*Downton Abbey*

I was recently watching the movie *The New Adventures of Pippi Longstocking* (1988) with my daughters. I grew up watching this movie and it brought back so many memories! I smiled when Tommy and Annika, the two children who lived next door to Pippi, heard noises one night from Pippi's house and decided to investigate. They quietly hopped out of bed to sneak from the house and see what was going on. What amused me about this? The brother and sister took the time to put dressing gowns on over their pajamas.

A dressing gown lets you modestly cover up your pajamas while still looking stylish. The concept of a dressing gown might seem passé, especially now that it's a fashion trend to wear flannel pajama bottoms in public. Just yesterday in town

I saw a woman walking down the sidewalk in her pajamas. This is the strangest phenomenon. She didn't look as if she'd locked herself out of the house or was running from a fire. She looked as if she was going about her business . . . *in pajamas*. I actually can't imagine being in a public place in my pajamas. For me it would be like the proverbial nightmare, in which you are out shopping and realize you have no pants on.

Our preschool has an annual pajama day. My daughters love this day because it's such a novelty to wear their pj's to school with all of their friends. As I walked them home after pajama day, we came upon a woman walking her dog. The woman remarked on how cute the girls looked. My older daughter proudly told her it was "pajama day" at school. Then there was a moment of silence before she asked the lady, "Is it pajama day for you too?" You guessed it: the woman was in her pajamas in the middle of the day. You know me with awkward moments, I wished the lady a good day and we were out of there faster than you could say "maladroit!" Wearing a dressing gown is the exact opposite of wearing your pajamas in public. You are covering your pajamas up and you are doing it stylishly.

Dressing gowns serve dual purposes: to keep you warm

and also to keep you decent. Madame Chic always wore a dressing gown. She had a quilted zip-up gown that she wore in the winter, as well as a kimono-style gown for the summer. In fact, I never saw her in her actual pajamas because that would have been inappropriate! If you're wearing especially revealing sleepwear, with sheer or thin fabric, it's always a good idea to wear a dressing gown. Your children do not want to see Mommy in a sexy nightgown. Neither do your houseguests. When you are staying overnight as a guest in someone's home, you should always have a dressing gown to cover your nightgown in case someone should come to your door or you have to walk down the hall to the bathroom. The exception to this is if you wear button-down or loungewear-style pajamas. But even so, you can wear a robe on top if you'd like to feel more comfortable traipsing off to the kitchen for a midnight snack.

You do not need to own several dressing gowns—one or two will be sufficient. When you dress well at night, a dressing gown is the finishing touch.

❧ What to Wear: ❧
Special Circumstances

Having poise means being properly dressed for every occasion. If you are dressed properly, you will be comfortable and confident. Here are a few fashion guidelines to consider for special occasions.

Touring Paris (or any city)

You are probably going to be on a vacation in the summer, when it is hot. Of course you want to be comfortable, but you are not going to a beach. You will be a visitor in someone else's home, which is likely a cultural and business capital of the world. A person with poise shows respect by dressing appropriately. Be sure to wear good walking shoes. Yes, if that means tennis shoes for you, then wear them; however, there are many flat shoes that are also comfortable, great to walk in, and stylish. Flip-flops are not good walking shoes. Your feet will be filthy in an hour. Also avoid T-shirts, shorts, sneakers, fanny packs, and baseball hats. On a hot day, a nice dress or tailored shorts and a cool blouse will be equally comfortable and more chic. Don't be surprised if you blend right in with the locals and people start speaking to you in their native tongue! Always remember to bring a layering piece in case you are out all day and the weather changes. Get excited about the challenge of coming up with an outfit that is equally comfortable and more fashionable. Check out the local style customs and try them out for yourself! Wear a scarf like that Parisian woman, drape a sweater around your shoulders like that elegant Italian lady. When in Rome, or anywhere else for that matter, respect and experience the culture by emulating the local style.

To a wedding

The standard rule holds true that a guest should not wear white to a wedding unless otherwise specified in the invitation or by dress-code decree. You cannot go wrong by selecting an elegantly tasteful dress that is not too revealing. Nothing too short or low-cut. You may wear a hat or fascinator if appropriate. For footwear, keep the venue in mind. If the wedding takes place on a beach or in a garden, for example, you will want to avoid heels. Here is a mini-guide to decode the dress code:

Formal or black tie. You can wear an elegant floor-length gown or a tasteful evening cocktail dress. Evening makeup and bold jewelry are perfectly acceptable.

Cocktail attire. Choose a cocktail dress in darker colors for evening and lighter colors for a day wedding. Heels, special jewelry, and a pretty hairdo will round out the look. Make sure your cocktail dress is flattering but not too sexy. Avoid seriously low-cut necklines or miniskirt hemlines.

Dressy casual. A cocktail dress or a tailored suit is appropriate, as are a skirt and chic blouse worn with heels. Keep from looking too casual by doing something special with your hair such as a chic chignon, bun, or Old Hollywood wave.

Beach wedding. Bohemian looks work really well here—a sundress or maxi dress with flat sandals, for example. Let your hair down or wear it half-up, half-down, with flowers behind your ear. Makeup can be natural and appropriate for daytime.

Casual. If the wedding indicates that the dress code is casual, still put something special into your appearance. A sundress, or a casual suit (skirt or pants), and tasteful makeup are totally appropriate.

To a funeral

Black, navy, or other somber colors are appropriate for a funeral. Make sure the outfit is not too revealing and displays respect. Nothing too flashy, too short, or too low-cut. No jeans. Think conservative.

To the theater

The performance you are about to see has been prepared with much care and artistry and deserves respect. Dress accordingly. Wear something special to the theater whether you are seeing a local play, a ballet, an opera, or listening to a symphony. You would feel wrong strolling into the Dorothy Chandler Pavilion in your flip-flops and ripped shorts (hopefully you don't own ripped shorts anyway!), for example. Use your intuition to tell you how to dress. If you're going to opening night at the ballet, wear something a little dressier than you would if you are seeing a local play at the community center. Either way, add something special to your outfit. If you are attending an artistic production right after work, put on lipstick, drape a shawl around your shoulders, or switch out your earrings. Do something to differentiate this outfit from your daily attire, to signify that you are experiencing something special. Have a few outfits in your extras or a few ways to dress up your core pieces that are effortless and well-thought-out outfits for the theater. This way, you will never be in a bind and wondering what to wear. Think about it while you're planning your wardrobe and maybe it will inspire you to seek out the arts even more than you already do!

To a fancy event

Every woman should have one or more dressy outfits in the extras section of her closet. You could have a little black dress that is useful for any occasion, from a date night to opening night at the theater. You could have a beautiful silk dress that might be worn to a wedding or to an anniversary party. You could have a pretty cocktail dress that would be perfect for a holiday fete or a charity benefit. If you regularly attend fancy events, it's a great idea to have a small capsule collection of occasion wear that you can pull from. Don't be shy about wearing the same dress twice. Take a cue from Catherine, the Duchess of Cambridge, who frequently repeats the same outfits but changes the way she accessorizes them or the way she wears her hair. If you follow me on social media, you'll see pictures from my events, and I will wear the same fancy dresses over and over, just in different ways. My work calls for many such special events, whether I'm speaking to an audience or giving fashion commentary on television. Plus I am a frequent patron of the arts, so a small collection of fancy dresses is a necessity for me.

FOR PANTY HOSE

The basic rule for panty hose is to either make it look as if you aren't wearing any at all or to use them as a fashion accessory, as with an opaque tight. Panty hose sure have come a long way. Sheer panty hose in a "nude" color that matches your skin can do wonders for evening out the skin tone on your legs. They can hide any unsightly bruises, scratches, or unwanted hair, and give the illusion of toned and taut legs. Who wouldn't want that? Forget the ill-matched nudes of the eighties, panty hose are available in a multitude of shades, and you are sure to find one that is the perfect "nude" for your skin tone. If you are not going for sheer nude, make your hose another accessory by wearing sheer or opaque black tights.

Day-to-night style

If you will be going out on the town after a long day at the office, it's a good idea to have a few tricks up your sleeve to be able to transition from day to night style. Simply switch out your accessories to make the subtle transition. Here are a few ideas:

Replace your flats with heels. Carry the unworn shoes in your handbag or keep a pair of extra shoes in your office.

Change out your jewelry and wear something more "evening."

Update your lipstick or darken up your eye shadow.

Convert your scarf into a shawl over your shoulders.

Plan to wear a fabulous dress to work covered by a blazer or cardigan. When ready to go out, simply remove the top layer.

Clothing is not merely for covering ourselves. It should never be an afterthought. Our clothing and, as an extension, our style, should be intentional. Our clothing choices communicate so much about us to the world. The way we dress represents our state of mind and our verve for life. If our clothes are sloppy, our presentation is sloppy. Something is off. But if we get into the groove of looking presentable no matter the circumstances and expressing our unique style while doing so, we are not only looking good, but we are revealing our poise.

Chapter 4

GLORIOUS GROOMING

Grooming is key to presenting yourself well. Poise is impossible unless you look clean and neat. If you are well groomed, you tell the world that you feel you are worth care and attention—from yourself and others. In a society where many women pile their messy hair on top of their head, display weeks-old chipped nail polish, and wear old workout clothes covered in dog hair, grooming is becoming a lost art. Really, it is a basic necessity.

Good grooming is about paying attention to the details of your physical appearance. If you stick to regular grooming routines and keep them simple, you can keep yourself always looking clean and polished, no matter how bad your day is going or how little sleep you got.

⚌⁓ Hair ⁓⚌

When it comes to hair, you not only need a cut that works best for your lifestyle, but you also need a game plan on how and when you are going to take care of your hair. Avoid long locks or extensions if you don't have the time to keep them up. If you have a lifestyle that requires a very low-maintenance beauty routine, consider a no-nonsense shorter hairdo. Madame Chic did not have hours to blow-dry her hair, so she had a very short Parisian bob. So did her daughter. If your hair does not tend to get dirty and you can get away with washing it less as I can (I wash mine twice a week), then you can have longer hair. I blow-dry mine twice a week and have set aside time to do that. I have also incorporated time-saving routines to keep my hair generally looking nice. I often post on Instagram my "bad hair day quick fixes." These are handy for all women to have.

You know your hair better than anyone, yes, even better than your hairstylist. You know your schedule; you know how much time you have in the morning to get ready; you know how often you need to wash it; you know how you like to wear it and what it will ideally look like. Whatever your hair is like, it should always look neat and clean, and it should be styled so that others can see your eyes and face. If you color your hair, plan a regular schedule of appointments so that your roots are not neglected. Have your hair cut every six to eight weeks.

For the days when you are very pressed for time, aren't feeling well, or are having a really bad hair day, have a few default hairstyles that you can accomplish with little effort and little time. YouTube is full of these hair tutorials, and I have many of them on my channel.

When in doubt, simply use a good hairbrush to smooth out your hair. Whether you do this and wear it down, or tie it back into a ponytail or simple bun, brushing your hair (unless you have naturally curly hair) is a grooming method that takes very little time and goes a long way to adding poise to your appearance.

NO-HEAT OVERNIGHT WAVES

If I want to cut back on blow-drying my hair, I always go for this overnight trick: Before bedtime, brush your hair several times, until it is smooth and tangle-free. Then spray a lightweight hair spray all over your hair. Now French braid your hair in pigtails (two braids, on either side of your head). Secure the ends with an elastic, as close to the end of the braids as possible. Get a good night's sleep. When you wake up, take out the braids and enjoy the lovely heat-free waves you've created.

Easy tips for chic hair:

• Create a deep side part in your hair (different than where you normally part your hair). Brush it down with a comb that has a tiny amount of hair spray on it. Secure it into a low ponytail (hide the elastic by wrapping a small amount of hair around it and pinning it into place with bobby pins), or secure it into a bun and hide the scraggly ends. Creating this deep part will prevent any frizzy flyaways.

- Speaking of flyaways, tame them by spraying hair spray on a new toothbrush (that you will clearly only use for this task) and brushing the flyaways down. This is very handy for the "sideburns" in front of the ears.

- Revisit the half-up hairstyle. Brush the top half of your hair back away from your face. Bring it to the middle of the back of your head and twist. Secure four times with bobby pins in a crisscross fashion. Spray with hair spray if needed.

- To perk up a listless ponytail, prop it up with bobby pins. Brush your hair back and secure it into a high ponytail with an elastic. Flip your hair over and on the bottom of the elastic, place two bobby pins, facedown, ridges facing inward, to prop up the ponytail higher.

⟿ Nails ⟿

Think clean, whether you have a painted manicure or not. Painted nails aren't for everyone, and many women just like to have healthy bare nails. If you love nail color, empower yourself to do your manicures at home. Even if you can afford to go to a nail salon each week, you should still know how to give yourself a manicure so you can fix any chips that may appear. Once your nail polish looks old and starts to chip, be sure to take it off. It's better to have no nail polish on than chipped nail polish. If you work in customer service or retail, where people can see your hands, well-groomed nails are a must. If you are going for a job interview or would like to make a great impression on people, you have got to have clean nails, polished or not.

I used to rely on getting manicures and pedicures from the salon. It was a regular trip for me every two weeks. I told myself I couldn't do them myself—(especially the pedicures!), that they would never look as good as the salon job. When I was looking to cut down my spending budget each month, manicures and pedicures were the first things to go.

I was really surprised to see a YouTube video from TV star Lo Bosworth that said she never got professional manicures and pedicures—she always did them herself, even for red carpet events! Sometimes you just need to hear this from other people to make you ask yourself what the heck is holding you back. I thought if she could do her own nails for red carpet events, I could surely do mine too! After much practice, I am happy to say that I produce salon-quality manicures and pedicures.

Even if you do not paint your nails, keep on top of grooming them. Never let your nails get too long or allow them to be uneven lengths. Cut with clippers if necessary and then file. Always keep a nail file handy in case you ever snag or break a nail. Take care of your feet by regularly buffing the hard calluses on the heels and pads. Moisturize your feet on a daily basis to avoid cracked heels. At least once a week, before bed, apply a heavy cream and then wear thick socks while you sleep. You will wake up to moisturized and soft feet.

⌒ Brows ⌒

Do you want an instant makeover? Get your brows groomed! When you "clean up" the brow area by shaping them into the perfect frame for your face, you transform your entire look. I still don't understand how a few plucked hairs can have so much impact, but they do. It's a great idea to consult a professional when you are having your brows groomed for the first time or if you are trying to correct years of incorrect plucking. Brow trends go in and out. Just think of the thin, high arches of the silent films stars of the thirties vs. Brooke Shields's or Cara Delevingne's thick brows. My advice is to never go too thin. I think a nice healthy brow frames the face, and sometimes when you over-pluck the hair never grows back. Oh, why can't it be like this on other areas of the body? (You know the ones I mean.)

When grooming your brows, you can choose between tweezing, threading, and waxing. I go to a threading salon near my house. These ladies are experts! My brows come out great every time. When I sit in the chair, I just ask them to "clean them up" rather than go through an overhaul. They just follow the shape of my natural arch and clean up the stragglers. A well-groomed brow line helps you look neat and clean.

If you are grooming your own brows, it's important to find the start and end points. For each eyebrow, hold a pencil vertically in front of your face. Line the pencil up from outer side of your nostril and up the bridge of your nose. The inner edge of the eyebrow should align with the top of the bridge of your nose. The height of the eyebrow's arch can be determined by placing the pencil on the outer edge of the nostril. This time, fan the pencil out so that it crosses the iris of your eye (make sure you are looking forward). Where the top of the pencil hits should be the position of highest point of the eyebrow's arch. With a tweezer, pluck any hairs below this area. Find the outside end of each eyebrow by aligning the bottom of the pencil with the outer edge of your nostril, then fanning out the pencil to the outer corner of the eye, creating a diagonal line. If you shape your brows and feel you have made an error, allow your brows to grow out as much as possible and then seek a professional to help get them back on track.

⸺ Unwanted Hair ⸺

Unwanted hair. The scourge of many a woman's grooming regime. Why can't those difficult-to-grow eyebrow hairs set the example for leg, armpit, bikini, and upper lip hair? Oh well, they don't, so we need to figure out how to groom these areas. Poise is in the details.

There are many hair removal options on the market: waxing, shaving, threading, bleaching, and even laser hair removal. When deciding how to tame the hairiness, you need to keep in mind a few things: budget, pain tolerance, and long-term vs. short-term results. I have tried nearly everything on the market, and although I might not be maintaining my air of mystery, I am very happy to share my results with you (all in the name of chicness, of course).

I shave my legs, thread my eyebrows, and have had my upper lip, armpits, and bikini line treated with laser hair removal. This system has worked for me. I used to wax the bikini, underarm, and upper lip, but it was painful and needed to be done too frequently, so I decided to invest in laser hair removal in these pesky areas. While laser hair removal does not remove the hair forever, it can significantly reduce the hair growth and thus reduce said peskiness. I shave my legs probably three times a week with a razor and ladies' shaving cream, and every three to four weeks I get my brows threaded. There, now you know it all. Whatever method you choose, find one that works for your wallet and your sanity.

Teeth

Whenever I travel outside of the United States, I often hear people remarking about how so-and-so has "American teeth." "What are American teeth?" I once asked someone in England. "Straight, white and shiny!" was the reply. Well, I did take that as a compliment. We do like keeping our teeth in top form over here. I suffered for my "American teeth" as a youth by wearing braces on and off for eight years (!) to correct my crooked, gapped, and bucktoothed smile (I thank my parents now, but at the time I was not amused). And while having straight teeth is nice, they certainly do not have to be straight to be pretty. Clean and healthy will suffice. The

American Dental Association recommends you brush your teeth at least twice a day and floss every evening.

If you are looking for pearly whites, there are many teeth whiteners on the market, from the drugstore varieties to the expensive procedures at the dentist's office. I just try not to let my front teeth touch soda, wine, or coffee. If, as I am, you are the sort who grinds your teeth or thrusts your tongue against your teeth while sleeping, you can consider getting a nighttime or even permanent retainer to avoid getting jagged or crooked teeth. No matter what your teeth look like, never be too shy to give a big toothy grin. Poised people never hide their smile. They embrace it because it embraces others.

Scent

To wear or not to wear a scent, that is the question. I am a big advocate for having a signature scent or two—fragrances that people know you for. My signature scents are Jo Malone Blackberry & Bay and Stella. If I want the fragrance to be light and subtle, I will apply just the scented body cream. If I would like it to be stronger, I will spritz the perfume too. Or I'll spritz the perfume and not use the cream. It's lovely to wear perfume, and I am fascinated by why people are drawn to certain fragrances. You might love floral fragrances, while your friend might like a clean, citrus scent. Your neighbor likes woodsy, spicy scents, while your sister likes more verdant fragrances. What family of scents are you drawn to? Most likely you'll like one that it is directly linked to your personal style. If you have a romantic, feminine style, you might be drawn to floral fragrances with notes of rose and lilac. If you have more of a bohemian style, you might like patchouli, coriander, or woodsy notes. Sporty types might like the fresh notes of citrus or marine essence.

When wearing scent, however, you must always take other people into consideration. One of my dear friends, an actress, does not like scent as it makes her feel nauseous. One time at an awards show, she went into the ladies' room, where a fellow actress was spraying herself with perfume in front of the mirror. Upon seeing my friend, this actress gave her a warm embrace, which is nice, except that my poor friend felt nauseous the rest of the evening as she reluctantly wore the other actress's perfume.

If you are going to be in close quarters with people—a long car or plane ride, or a classroom environment, for example, it's a good idea not to wear any scent at all or, if you do, to keep it very light. I'm not sure if Madame Chic had a signature scent, because I was never close enough to her to smell it. Some people are wearing so much perfume that you know what scent they are wearing before they even walk in the room! This is too much. Keep in mind that you get used to the perfume you wear and stop smelling it after a while, so keep going light on the application.

ETIQUETTE TIP—PERFUME
AND *LES BÉBÉS*

Avoid wearing heavy perfume when you are going to visit a new baby. The most well-intentioned visitors have no idea that their heavy dose of Spicebomb is what is actually making that cute baby sneeze.

~ Makeup ~

A vital element to cultivating poise is to present your best self, and always strive to *be* your best self. You should not hide yourself behind anything, especially too much makeup. A poised woman should use makeup to polish and enhance her natural beauty. And while we might have fun experimenting with a bold lip color or a smoky eye shadow, it's a good idea to remember not to hide who we are. When you see a poised woman, you notice her naturalness, her confidence, the way you feel at ease around her, that attractive quality that is rather magnetic. Poised women don't look as if they are hiding something.

Have you ever been assisted by a makeup artist at a department store who was wearing so much makeup that you wondered if you could trust her judgment? When cultivating poise in our appearance, we do not want people to notice our makeup before they notice anything else about us. We do not want people to meet us and question our judgment. This is not to say that we cannot experiment with makeup or even try out some trends. The point, however, in experimenting with makeup is to "bring out your eyes" or "enhance your high cheekbones" or "draw attention to your smile." So if you are going to experiment with makeup, keep these things in mind. We are not trying to win any fan girl contests; we are trying to enhance our natural beauty. The most beautiful thing is our natural self. Don't let your eyes get lost behind those extreme lashes. Don't let your smile get eclipsed behind the dark lip liner. Don't let your cheekbones become ambushed by your complicated contouring routine. Start from scratch if need be and scrap your entire makeup routine. On this journey to cultivate poise, there are many familiar activities that we will have to change, no matter how long we have been doing them.

The Madame Chic beauty philosophy centers around *le no-makeup look*, which should be a quick daily routine that you can pull off effortlessly and can feel confident with in public. I cannot count how many times this *le no-makeup look* has come in handy for me. When I am running late, not feeling my best, or have plans that change drastically at the last minute, I am still able to get ready quickly and go through my day with confidence because I took a few minutes in the morning to apply natural, beauty-enhancing makeup. Of course I don't have to wear makeup to feel confident, but, like putting on my nice clothes, it does do a little something to boost my morale.

MY 5-MINUTE *LE NO-MAKEUP* LOOK

After moisturizing my skin and applying SPF, I dab on tinted moisturizer, BB cream, or a foundation with my fingers or a beautyblender. I cover my under-eye circles with a brightening concealer and quickly do spot coverage, if needed, with a full-cover concealer over any blemishes or sun spots. I set everything with powder. I fill in my eyebrows with a powder. I apply burgundy mascara (a favorite color to bring out the green in my eyes). I apply blush to the tops of my cheekbones and to finish off, apply lip gloss.

This routine take five minutes or less. Create a five-minute routine that works for you, and that allows you to look your best. Take a "before" and "after" picture and see what a difference your *le no-makeup* routine makes. Decide if it's worth it to use it on a regular basis. You might never have worn makeup and don't feel the need to wear it. I once had a college student ask me if she should start wearing makeup because she never had before. I told her no, not unless she wanted to. Some women have naturally defined features and don't need to wear makeup. I know several women like this and they are very fortunate!

Of course, if I have more time or a desire to do something different, I might wear eye shadow and eyeliner, but with the guideline that they always look natural and not too heavy.

Feeling comfortable in their skin is a big part of that *je ne sais quoi* that poised people possess. We will aim to take great care of our skin (more on this in a moment), but no matter how well we take care of our skin, sometimes age, sun spots, hormonal breakouts, or interrupted sleep affect the way our skin looks. Enter foundation. If you pick the right one for you, you can even out your skin tone and cover a multitude of problems.

Different types of foundations

BB cream. The BB in BB cream stands for beauty balm. These are multifunctional creams that offer many benefits in one product. BB creams are becoming a favorite among many women because they cover so many skin-care steps in one go. Many BB creams contain sun protection coverage, anti-aging properties, moisturizers, skin-smoothing components, and color coverage. The BB cream is my go-to coverage when I am in a hurry or am having a casual day.

Tinted moisturizer. If you do not like wearing heavy foundation, a tinted moisturizer will do the trick. It provides light coverage and often includes an SPF. For those women with scarring or dark spots, however, tinted moisturizer might not be enough to even out the skin tone.

Liquid foundation. For those who require heavier coverage, you can't go wrong with good old-fashioned liquid foundation. Depending on the amount of coverage you need, you can find everything from light to heavy formulas. There are thousands of brands and so many to choose from, so it's a great idea to meet with a makeup artist and try a few for yourself. Have your color professionally matched so that it blends in flawlessly with your natural skin. I always depend on liquid foundation if I am doing an event, plan on being photographed, or need my makeup to look good all day long.

Mineral foundation. Mineral foundation is great for women who have sensitive skin and are looking for natural ingredients in their makeup. Often found in powder form, mineral foundation can provide flawless *le no-makeup look* coverage. It is usually applied with a brush.

Modes of application

Depending on the type you use, there are many methods with which to apply foundation. You can use your fingers, a makeup brush, a sponge, or a beautyblender. If you use a beautyblender or similar product to apply your foundation, remember to dampen the beautyblender before application. Then dot the foundation on your skin and apply using the beautyblender in circular motions, or put some liquid foundation on the back of your hand, dab the damp beautyblender in the foundation, and apply. Women who are interested in more high-tech makeup application can try out an airbrush machine. These at-home devices provide impeccable foundation coverage. You place a little bit of liquid foundation into the nozzle and spray it lightly over your face. The application is so even and precise, you'll never have any harsh lines. I've had my makeup professionally airbrushed for television appearances as well as photo shoots and have always been impressed with the results! Airbrush machines require more maintenance and will need to be cleaned out after each use. Brushes and sponges will need to be cleaned with a cleanser every few days.

Make it stay

No matter what kind of foundation you choose, if you want it to last all day, use either a primer before applying your makeup or a setting spray after application.

⌇ Skin Care ⌇

Sure we have developed a makeup routine that makes our face look flawless, but it always helps to be working on a prime canvas. We need to take care of our skin. There are so many factors that can lead to problem skin: stress, diet, bad habits like smoking and tanning, hormones, sleep deprivation, too much caffeine. You name it and it might affect the skin! The good news is that as you start to develop poise, you will know how to handle many things that might pop up and cause you stress (more on this in the latter half of the book). Working on yourself inside and out will, believe it or not, help your skin! You won't be tempted to eat all of that greasy junk food because you will become more conscious about what you eat. You will slow down during the day and focus more on what matters. You will develop your inner confidence and move through sticky situations with grace. The things that used to make your skin look haggard in the past will no longer be an issue. That said, we still need to take care of our skin!

Come up with a skin-care routine that works for you. The main things to remember are: do not overcleanse your skin in the morning (all I do is splash warm water on my face, then apply moisturizer and SPF before applying makeup . . . it's my number one skin-care tip!), and thoroughly remove your makeup in the evening. I like to use makeup removal wipes and eye-makeup remover before cleanser and exfoliation. Pick a moisturizing cream that works for your skin as well as an eye cream and lip hydration. Get or give yourself regular facials. Getting plenty of rest (go to bed early!), drinking water, deep breathing through tough situations, and having many still moments throughout the day also help immensely.

Proper grooming is the necessary punctuation mark on our appearance. It communicates that we have the self-respect to treat and display ourselves with dignity. That we take the time to care. This attention to detail is an important component of poise.

Chapter 5

DAPPER DEPORTMENT

Poise is about how we present ourselves. Yes, style, clothes, makeup, and grooming are important aspects of the way we look. But there's another factor that influences the way others see us. You could even say it's the most important. Deportment is defined as "the way a person behaves, stands, or moves." You can be the most stylishly dressed, beautifully coiffed woman in town, but if you don't have good deportment, you'll still be, in the words of my grandmother, "mutton dressed as lamb."

⌒ Posture ⌒

Elegance is usually confused with superficiality, fashion, lack of depth. This is a serious mistake: human beings need to have elegance in their actions and in their posture because this word is synonymous with good taste, amiability, equilibrium and harmony.

—Paulo Coelho

Posture is physical poise. It is a physical manifestation of where we are in our day: Frazzled? Overwhelmed? Exhausted? Throwing in the towel? Defeated? Anxious? You might not need to tell anyone you're feeling these things; they probably already know just by looking at your posture.

When you are in the midst of a difficult situation, notice how you hunch over. Notice how tightly your shoulders are clenched. Notice how your neck juts out. Notice the collapsed feeling you get in your core muscles. When you notice these things, let them be a reminder to bring yourself back to poise. Strengthen those core muscles. Breathe deeply to disperse the tension. Roll those shoulders down. Hold that head high. If you correct your posture, you'll feel the strength of poise. Now you have the power to defeat your difficulties.

What if you aren't going through anything tough but you just naturally default to bad posture? Perhaps you sit at a computer for several hours each day and your natural tendency is to hunch over. I played the saxophone in the high school marching band. The strap that held the heavy saxophone tugged my neck forward. So many years later I am still correcting my learned tendency to jut my neck out all the time.

Make a commitment to becoming aware of your posture. After sitting at the computer for a long time, stand up and roll your arms backward to reverse the hunched over effect. Make an effort to sit up straight as you work. Bring this awareness to everything you do. Notice your weakness. When you're tired, are you more inclined to slouch? When you are stressed, do you resort to shallow breathing and pinching your shoulders together? When you notice your bad habits, take a breath and concentrate on reversing them.

Posture during mealtime is especially important. Food just tastes better when you are enjoying it with excellent posture. Try eating dinner hunched over with your stomach muscles collapsed. It's an unpleasant feeling. The food feels as if it's all flowing into a mushy pit—your stomach! I catch myself slouching at the dinner table all the time. Usually when I sit down for a meal, I'm exhausted from working, cooking, and cleaning. I just want to collapse into my chair for a brief rest while I eat. But posture here is critical. With good posture, you will become more aware of what you are eating and how much you are eating. You will feel more social and more inclined to engage in conversation. By sitting up straight, you will elevate the elegance of your meal. And, most important, you will be providing a good example for your family as they notice how elegantly you eat.

The unexpected benefits of good posture

Good posture will encourage you to make better choices about everything from the clothes you wear in the morning, to how you deal with sass from your child, to how you eat your dinner. When you stand before your wardrobe in the morning to choose your outfit for the day and you do so with excellent posture, you are less likely to go for the baggy sweatpants. You will want to dress yourself beautifully to match your new gracefulness. When your child's behavior is particularly out of control, you are more likely to handle it in a levelheaded way if you maintain your posture and quiet breath. Your posture will be a physical reminder that you are the adult and you need to handle the situation with maturity and wisdom. You are less likely to snack on handfuls of cheese crackers when you have excellent posture. Just watch the benefits accrue when you simply stand up straight.

Guide to good posture

With an exercise let's remind ourselves of why we're doing this. Stand up right now and try to have *bad* posture. You'll notice that your shoulders lean forward, your chin hangs down, your stomach juts out, your pelvis tilts forward, your knees lock, and your chest collapses. If you stand like this long enough, you will get the sensation that gravity is pulling you down even more than it normally does! It's a very heavy feeling.

Now it's time to experience the lightness of excellent posture.

Unhunch your shoulders by moving them back and down your back. Feel how this makes your chest feel expansive rather than constricted. Lift up your chin and tuck it in as your straighten your head. If it helps, picture a string pulling your head up from its center. Pull the core muscles of your abdomen in. Tuck your pelvis in slightly. Straighten your back.

Relax your arms and knees. Notice how much lighter you feel. It is easier to breathe. So much changes in this instant. You feel as though you can conquer anything! This is a lot to remember, I know! But if you practice this every morning when you first get out of bed, eventually it will come naturally to you and will be your default posture. Anything less than this will feel uncomfortable.

POSTURE EXERCISE

For the rest of the day be very conscious of your posture. Make it one of the primary things you think about. Exaggerate your good posture by walking elegantly, as though you are channeling Grace Kelly. Notice how this change in your posture affects other areas of your life. You might feel as if you are doing "play pretend" because it's simply not who you are. It might feel formal and thus unnatural compared to how you are used to carrying yourself, but keep it up until the very end of the day.

A tendency to lean

One of my bad posture habits is to lean against things. The minute I walk up to a counter, I lean against it—whether I'm cooking or at the bank teller's window. Avoid leaning on things for support, and stand up straight, as though you are strong enough to support yourself.

A BALLERINA'S SECRET
TO GOOD POSTURE

I had the great pleasure of asking Allyssa Bross, principal dancer for the Los Angeles Ballet, what a ballerina's secret to great posture is. Here is what she said:

Many times ballet dancers are known for their great posture, and automatically people assume it is because they stand with their shoulders back and spine straight, but posture is more than the way one stands. Posture is the way one carries oneself in any social setting. It starts from within, and then moves outward.

Controlling one's body and posture starts with the mind. Thoughts affect our actions, body, and the way we take care of it. Here are five helpful tips to keep good posture:

1. Loving yourself
2. Confidence
3. Exercise (When you have strong, nimble muscles, posture is easier to maintain.)
4. Chin up and neck long
5. Eye contact

Walking

Now let's take our good posture and go for a stroll. How do you walk? Have you ever thought about this before? Do you take long strides or short choppy steps? Is your natural tendency to clomp or glide when you walk? I'm a clomper. I clomp around the house. I clomp up the stairs. I clomp down the stairs. A clomp is a rather ungraceful way of walking. You walk with purpose and determination, but your feet fall heavily on the ground. Horses clomp. People shouldn't. When I committed to cultivating poise, I knew I had to stop clomping and start gliding. When you walk as though gliding, your feet are light, your posture fluid, and your movements graceful. You can still walk with purpose and determination, but in an elegant manner. Gliding is being light on your feet. It is preventing the weight of your body slamming to the floor with every step. Walking gracefully requires lifted posture and ease of step. We are still going to get where we're going but we'll feel as if we are floating rather than sinking.

Walking in heels

Walking gracefully in high heels can be very tricky. Many women take short, choppy steps and perpetually look like they are about to tip forward. To avoid this, make sure you walk heel to toe rather than toe to heel. The natural tendency is to put your toes down first, as they are closer to the ground. Placing your heel before your toe gives your step more stability. You will need to utilize your good posture while also leaning slightly back. Take shorter steps than you would if you were wearing flats, but compensate for this by walking slower. Take a moment to put your heels on and practice walking around the house.

If you feel that you never will be comfortable in high heels, try something in a mid- or low-heel range. Madame Chic never wore high heels. The highest heels she wore were around two inches. On average, her shoes had a small heel of about one inch. If you feel more comfortable walking in lower heels, go for it. In my small shoe collection, I have more low-heeled shoes than high- for this very reason.

How to Behave Toward Others

Deportment isn't just posture. It is also behavior. How do you behave toward others? Do you ignore them? If you are poised and have good deportment, you are an open and accommodating member of society.

Walking in Public

There are a few etiquette tips to remember when walking in public:

When walking in a residential neighborhood, it's polite to greet your neighbors with either a kind word, a nod, or a smile.

Always walk to the right of the sidewalk to avoid that awkward side-step dance when you encounter an oncomer.

Avoid texting and walking at the same time lest you smack into a parking meter. If you must text, pull off to the side, complete your text, and then keep walking.

Do not obstruct foot traffic by stopping in the middle of the sidewalk, at the top of an escalator, or as you exit an elevator, bus, or subway. Instead move to the side.

When you're outside, take in the sights, breathe in the fresh air, and appreciate your neighborhood. Be very aware of your surroundings, relax, and enjoy yourself. Even if you're just walking to run errands.

Handshake, hug, or *faire la bise*?

Depending on which country you are in, it's a good idea to be well versed in the appropriate way to greet people. In America we like a good, strong handshake. Simply hold out your right hand, and with a medium-firm grip (not too tight!) shake for two or three pumps, while maintaining eye contact, and then release. Never grip too tightly, especially if you are shaking an elderly person's hand, as they might suffer from painful arthritis.

Many European countries prefer the much more intimate cheek kiss, or *faire la bise*. Exchanging a cheek kiss for the first time can feel really awkward. It's so intimate! You're so close! There are many more nuances to the cheek kiss than there are to the handshake. First thing to know: you don't actually kiss the cheek! You do not want to leave a lipstick mark on your new acquaintance. Simply lean in and press your right cheek to theirs. You can make a kiss sound if you like but nothing too loud. When you lean in, you may touch the other person's shoulder or arm or elbow with one or both hands (so confusing, I know).

Okay, you've conquered the first cheek, and now comes the tricky minefield of figuring out if this person gives one or two kisses. I even met people in Paris who gave three kisses(!). Go slow when you are pulling away from the first kiss, to detect if your acquaintance is stepping back or going for the other cheek. Avoid any painfully awkward lip brushes (yes, these have happened to me, so embarrassing) by not pulling any fast movements.

Now what about the hug? We Americans like to hug our friends. But unless you are in America, avoid hugging people, even if you know them well. They simply do not know how to react. I remember I once greeted one of my husband's English friends whom I had known for several years. She is English and I'm American, and we were on the island of Tortola for a wedding, so the greeting etiquette lines were blurred. When I saw her for the first time, I leaned in for the cheek kiss and then embraced her in a hug (not sure where I concocted this hybrid of a greeting). As I embraced her tightly, she pulled away to kiss the other cheek. We ended up in a very awkward cuddling exchange that I would have preferred to avoid.

Eye contact

What happened to eye contact? It sometimes feels as if people just don't make eye contact anymore. We greet acquaintances without it. We ask questions of store clerks without it. We have entire exchanges with our colleagues without it. Younger people, especially, seem to prefer averting their gaze rather than looking into your eyes. Why is eye contact so intimidating?

Steady eye contact, much like a firm handshake, is an important component to good deportment and poise. Making eye contact is a sign of respect. Making eye contact is a sign of confidence. Making eye contact is a declaration that you have nothing to hide. Making eye contact communicates that you are trustworthy. Making eye contact when you are speaking to someone lets that person know you are listening to him or her.

If you are shy or introverted, making eye contact can feel excruciatingly awkward. This is because when we look into people's eyes, we see so much of them. Many philosophers have noted that the soul is laid bare in the eyes. If you struggle with making eye contact, it is a practice that you will need to cultivate. When you are talking with someone, look into that person's eyes not only as you are listening to the person, but also when you are talking to him or her. Remember to maintain steady breathing. The awkwardness will fade eventually, and you will begin to notice a very subtle power shift. You feel more powerful when you make eye contact with someone. It is truly liberating.

Have you ever been at a party when the person you were talking to was looking everywhere but you? Do you remember how you felt? When you focus your eyes on the person you're speaking to, you are in the moment. You are listening to that person. When you speak, maintain this eye contact.

You could be speaking to someone who also values eye contact, or you might be talking to someone who is uncomfortable with it and doesn't look at you. Either way, still look at that person's eyes. Don't compromise just because your conversation partner is struggling with eye contact. You will have a calming effect on this person, reassuring him or her that you are trustworthy and have nothing to hide. When you focus on another person at a party, it makes that person feel special and important. It has been written that this was part of the secret to Jackie Kennedy Onassis's charisma.

While you are talking to someone, feel free to look away; you don't need to lock gazes intensely for the duration of the conversation, but let your exchange be in the spirit of good eye contact.

Our behavior

Deportment isn't just standing tall, walking elegantly, and making eye contact, it is also about behavior. How do you behave toward others? Are you warm and friendly or bristly and brusque? If you are poised and have good deportment, you are an open and accommodating member of society. We can sometimes get so caught up in our own heads that we behave in an impolite or antisocial way. Let's make polite behavior a regular practice with the people we come in contact with in our daily lives. Because how we behave is very telling of where our values and priorities lie.

Good deportment must be extended to all corners of our lives, even when we are acting anonymously. Remember all of your actions affect the world for better or for worse. People who practice good behavior and deportment all day long but sit down at their computer at night writing mean comments on the internet, are not fully integrating poise into their lives. They don't yet see that all of their actions are important, not just the ones that are more publicly identifiable with them.

What about good deportment while driving? Let's say another driver honks at you on your nightly commute home. You have no idea what you have done to deserve to be honked at. You feel instant indignation. What is this person's problem? Can't this driver just be pleasant since we are all in this commute together? The other driver speeds in front of you and cuts you off. Now your indignation turns to rage. You feel tempted to put your foot on the accelerator and lay your hand on the horn. It would feel so good to give that crazy driver a hand gesture and to call him or her a name. You are about to get caught up in the moment, but good deportment stops you. You see that if you do these things you will be behaving just like this other driver. You will be lowering your standards. You have poise, and even though you've been slighted, you see the folly in starting a road argument during your commute. It's dangerous. It's not worth it. The other driver wants you to react. He or she wants you to be angry! That's what gives that driver satisfaction. You breathe through your anger and stay focused on the road as the other driver zips off to torment someone else. You did not let the behavior of this person lower the standards of your behavior. That is so much more satisfying in the long run.

It can feel triumphant to not stoop to poor behavior when dealing with someone who is behaving badly, but what about when we are in crowds of people with questionable behavior? Have you ever seen news footage from Black Friday or after-Christmas sales? People wake up at the earliest hours to wait in the dark and cold, only to storm the shops once the doors open, shoving one another left and right, and in some cases trampling on one another for discounted goods. Dignified people turn to animalistic behavior over objects. Fights will erupt over waffle makers. Tugs-of-war will ensue over a dollhouse. Where is the deportment? You've probably checked out pictures of these scenes with something between horror and amusement.

By putting their values and priorities in the right place, poised people set themselves up for success with regard to good deportment. Take, for example, Thanksgiving, a traditional American holiday. It is one of the loveliest celebrations of the year. Families gather around together at the table to feast and to give thanks. It is a holiday that has not been commercialized . . . yet. It emphasizes good food and strengthening relationships through gratitude. It used to be that most retail businesses closed on Thanksgiving Day in observance of the holiday. But recent trends have these retailers opening their doors Thanksgiving evening so that shoppers can get a head start on their bargain shopping. Families are abandoning the warm fireside of their homes to fight the crowds in their favorite store, and for what? *To acquire more stuff.* Their values and priorities are in the wrong place.

You never would have seen Madame Chic banging on the windows of Walmart, aching to get in for the Black Friday sales. Her good deportment would have not even allowed this behavior to be a possibility. You might feel tugged in the direction of participating in these consumer extravaganzas, and fret that you are missing out on a good deal. Here is where your poise comes in. A poised person knows her priorities. What is more important? A new blender at 50 percent off? Or spending quality time with your extended family as you give thanks? Would you rather play a board game by the fireplace long into the evening with your cousins? Or tussle with some lady in a shop over a discounted blow-dryer?

Poised people reject herd mentality. They don't think, Everyone else is doing it, so I should too. They avoid situations where people are behaving in a manner that is below their standards. They know that behavior is telling, and they want their behavior to inspire others to cultivate good deportment.

．　　．　　．

Let's begin to be conscious about our posture, our eye contact, the way we move, and the way we behave. Practicing good deportment is fun! And if you slip, just pick yourself right back up and try again. Soon your good deportment, one of the major building blocks of poise, will come to you like second nature.

Chapter 6

CHARMING

COMMUNICATION

The way we communicate, both verbally and nonverbally, speaks volumes about our character. Many of us get trapped in patterns of speech that do not match the level of poise we would like in our life. Let's dive right in and analyze how we talk. Because what we say and how we say it are far more powerful than we could ever know.

⟡ Speech ⟡

There is little you can do about the annoying speech mannerisms of

others, but there is a lot you can do
about your own.

—Emily Post

Good speech is a crucial component of poise. When you meet a well-spoken person, you instantly take note. That person sounds intelligent, levelheaded, and trustworthy. They have a certain *je ne sais quoi*. They appear to be straightforward and confident.

Being in Madame and Monsieur Chic's formal living room made me want to dress nicely and sit with good posture. Their formalities at the table made me want to brush up on my table manners and not slouch in my chair. The same thing can be said for being around any well-spoken person. Such a person makes us want to speak better. That person inspires us to use better vocabulary, eliminate filler words, vulgarities, and slang. He or she reminds us that we all have viewers and that if we are well-spoken, we can inspire the same quality in others.

Eliminating vulgarities

Poised people do not have potty mouth. If you struggle with this, and are committed to cultivating poise, it's time to clean up your language. I have not always been an angel in this area. When I was younger, I thought it was cool to swear and did so regularly when talking with my friends. Then after I observed how carefully Madame Chic always chose her words, swearing with my friends no longer felt funny to me, it just felt crass. When I decided to cultivate poise, I knew it had no place in my life. Cleaning up your language isn't always easy. I'm not promising that when I stub my toe an expletive won't come out of my mouth, but on the whole, I commit to being conscious about the words I speak.

When you commit to cleaning up your language, you might have to clean up the music you listen to and the entertainment you watch as well. The other day my husband and I decided to watch a popular detective show from a cable network because we had heard from many people that it was the "best show ever." We had to check it out! Twenty-five minutes into the first episode, I had to turn it off. My husband agreed. I don't care how brilliant a show is, I don't feel like listening to the f-bomb being dropped every ten seconds. Now that I've committed to cleaning up my language, listening to someone litter their speech with swear words is like watching a big black fly floating in a pretty china teacup. Perhaps this is why I like *Downton Abbey* so much? I'm sure that's one of many reasons.

So how can *you* deal with a society that increasingly devalues language and lauds the curse word? When I hear people cursing loudly in public, especially when I'm with my girls, I long to give the curser an etiquette smack-down. But I resist because I think setting a good example is more effective. You can commit to being a good example too. When you are at lunch with your friend who casually says the f-word repeatedly over salad and iced tea, you can commit to not joining in. You can commit to making all the sounds that come out of your mouth beautiful and empowering. Perhaps she will get it. Perhaps she won't. It doesn't matter. All that matters is that you are making a choice as to how your speech will affect the world. You have viewers, and they will be attracted to how intelligent and levelheaded you sound. Madame Chic never cursed. Nary a "*zut alors!*" came out of her mouth. She chose her words carefully, and now I choose to do the same.

"Um, like, totally."

Le sigh. Like and *um,* two scourges of modern communication. They plague my speech and (especially if you are of generation X or younger) most likely plague yours as well. If you are from Southern California, as I am, there might not be any hope for you (only kidding!). The curse of Valley girl slang has caused many of us to sound like bumbling airheads rather than the poised and intelligent people we are. So what can we do about it?

The first step is to be aware. Do you use "like" in every sentence? When you are not quite sure what to say, do you say "um" instead? Are you in your forties but when you talk still sound as if you're seventeen? When silence falls on a conversation, do you get anxious and ramp up the "likes" and "ums" even more? If, as I do, you suffer from Valley girl syndrome and pepper your speech with "like" and "um," ask yourself *pourquoi.*

Many people feel the need to fill any gaps in the conversation with mindless babble. A little bit of social anxiety might be behind all the "likes," "ums," and slang (more on this in a moment) we use. This is all in an attempt to fill the silence. The next time you are in a conversation with someone and the conversation lags, just observe your internal struggle. Why are you uncomfortable with silence? Why do you feel the need to fill the silence with chatter? What would happen if you just let the silence be and stayed there in the moment? Your whole body might be tense. You might feel very uncomfortable, but just ride it out. It's better to have silence than mindless babble, communicating in a way that isn't you. Silence also gives you time to reflect on what you are talking about.

I always knew I had a problem here, but the problem was really brought to my attention when I started to shoot and edit my YouTube videos. My goodness! I would drop "like" and "um" as if they were hot beignets! And I didn't even know I did it! It was only when reviewing the footage later that I noticed my lack of poise in speaking. Thankfully I was able to edit the "likes" and "ums" out of my videos, but we don't have that option in real time.

Become aware of the way you talk. If you feel nervous and are not sure what to say, it's better not to say anything than to use the empty filler "um." The same goes for "like."

Slang

The very first afternoon I met Monsieur and Madame Chic, Madame corrected my speech. I said "*j'sais pas*," which is a lazy slang way of saying, "I don't know" in French. Madame Chic, most likely horrified by visions of living for the next six months with a young woman who spoke French slang with an American accent, corrected me immediately. "*Je* ne *sais pas*, Jennifer," she said. Well that set the precedent, didn't it? I wouldn't be employing any slang words in this house! I'm glad she was direct with me on that first day rather than letting me go on making an un-poised fool of myself.

Younger people are always pushing the boundaries with slang, and the older you get, the more befuddled you might become with how they speak. I'm sure you've seen videos or television footage of young people who are supposedly speaking English but sound as if they are speaking a foreign language with their lack of grammar, proper sentence structure, and confusing slang. "Adorbs," "amazeballs," and "whaters" are like a secret code. It's fun to be in on the latest slang; it's a form of social currency among teens. But commit to speaking clearly, intelligently, and with poise. Your excellent diction will take you very far, I promise you. You will be favored at job interviews. You will attract intelligent, like-minded friends. You might find yourself in the wonderful position of mentoring young people who will look up to you. Your viewers will notice. So no matter how you spoke when you were younger, or how you talked yesterday or even this morning, you have the capacity to change. You possess the courage to clean up your language and to speak with clarity and intelligence. Your speech can be poised. Take charge of this area in your life and watch what doors become opened for you.

WAYS TO PRACTICE GOOD DICTION

Become an avid reader

Read classic literature

Learn a new word each day and use it in your speech

Listen to yourself when you speak

Eliminate vulgarities

Avoid excessive use of "like" and "um"

Avoid slang in most social situations but still remain au courant with the culture

Pause (and think!) before you speak

Become okay with silence

Listen to audiobooks and be inspired by the eloquent readers

If you're feeling nervous in a social setting, choose silence over mindless babbling

‿ Accept Compliments Graciously ‿

When someone gives me a compliment, I find it very difficult to simply say, "Thank you." When someone compliments you, are you inclined to deflect the compliment?

Do any of these sound familiar to you?

"You look beautiful today!"
"No way, I'm such a mess."

"Your hair looks lovely."
"That's because I actually washed it!"

"I love your dress."
"Oh, this old thing? I got it on clearance!"

Deflecting a compliment in this way is like rejecting a gift. If someone handed you a present, you wouldn't immediately hand it back and say, "No thanks!" When someone gives you the gift of a compliment, take that "present," open it, and say thank you.

Most of us have a self-deprecating nature. We don't want to boast. We don't want to appear vain. We don't want others to feel bad if we are doing better than they are. All of this is fine, but we don't have to put ourselves down in the process. If someone gives you a compliment, simply say, "Thank you."

"You look beautiful today!"
"Thank you!"

"Your hair looks lovely."
"Thank you!"

"I love your dress"
"Thank you!"

The truth is, the more you cultivate poise, the more compliments you will receive. People will notice something different about you. They won't quite be able to pinpoint how you've changed, but they will know that you have. You will appear confident. Mysterious. This will cause people to give you compliments. So get ready to say thank you. Your viewers are taking note.

∽ Saying No to Commitments ∽ with Poise

You are having a stressful day. You have a deadline at work. You feel as if you might be coming down with a cold. The mess in your home is something you don't even want to think about. There is nothing for dinner and you need to go to the grocery store, but you're not sure when you will fit in a trip. That morning while dropping off your child at school you run into a fellow parent and friend. She asks if you want to have a playdate later that afternoon. You have turned an invitation down from her in the past, and you didn't make her child's birthday party either because you were out of town. You feel bad about this. Even though you feel overwhelmed, you consider if you can fit the playdate in so you don't disappoint your friend. You know you should just say no, but you don't want to offend her. So you say yes. Then you go through your day wondering what on earth you were thinking agreeing to a playdate. You could go to the grocery store during that time! What will you do about dinner? You consider making an excuse to cancel. But you don't want to be known as one of those flaky people. Begrudgingly, you go on the playdate, but you know you should have just said no.

Saying no takes practice. Saying no with poise requires even more skill. How does one say no with poise? By learning how *not* to say no. One does not lie, or make unnecessary apologies or excuses. One does not allow room for guilt or shaming. Instead, one says no with grace and compassion and gentle firmness. The person you are saying no to might not be happy about it, and he or she might attempt to make you feel guilt, but you will be strong in your choice and not allow that to happen.

Only you know what is on your plate. You know the limits of your strength and endurance. Only you know what your schedule holds. Only you know how much sleep you got last night or what your top priorities are. Only you know how miserable you are when you overextend yourself. Therefore, only you can make a proper decision about whether to say yes or no to a potential commitment. Never allow someone to pressure you into something that your instinct tells you not to do.

If possible, say no immediately. A simple "no, thank you" will suffice. You do not need to give an excuse or tell a little white lie. The person you are saying no to will either accept your answer or not, but if he or she doesn't accept it, that is entirely that person's problem. Poised people avoid getting caught up in drama. Poised people are very straightforward and sure of themselves. No is a perfectly acceptable answer to any request.

POISED WAYS TO SAY NO

No, thank you.

I'm sorry, I'm going to have to decline.

That is not going to work for me.

I'm afraid I can't make it.

I cannot make it but thank you for inviting me.

My apologies but I cannot participate in this. Perhaps next time.

Thank you for thinking of me! I'm sorry I cannot attend.

What do you do when you have said yes to something when you really should have said no? Commitments are very important and should only be broken in serious circumstances. But broken they must be if they are going to test your safety, health, or overall mental well-being. Once one of my very good friends was throwing a party. I had made a commitment to come to the party. She lives about an hour away from me. As the time to leave for the party drew near, I approached it with dread because I was feeling exhausted and overwhelmed. My work schedule was huge, and I knew I'd need to work late into the night after I got home from the party to get it all done. I had gotten very little sleep the night before. I was coming off a week where my husband was out of town for six days and I hadn't had a break from being with the children. The thought of even getting in the car and driving twenty minutes was daunting, let alone driving two hours round-trip. But I didn't want to hurt my friend's feelings, so I carried on the charade of going. I tried to get the girls to put their shoes on, but they were being extra feisty that day and running around the house. As I chased after them for a few minutes, I saw the folly in all of this. What was I doing? I was completely exhausted and overwhelmed. I was in no position to go to this party. I suddenly knew what I had to do. I had to let my friend know that I wasn't coming. So I did. I told her the truth. I was exhausted and overwhelmed. The next day I also phoned her to apologize for not attending. She is a true friend and she understood. She was very gracious about it.

We can get caught up in not wanting to disappoint other people. We will go to great lengths to make sure our friends and acquaintances are pleased, but at what cost? I could have easily said that I, or one of my daughters, was ill. That would have gotten us off the hook instantly. But I don't want to have to lie to anyone, especially a friend. I should not have to tell a falsehood that merely perpetuates the people-pleasing cycle. The simple truth is always the best response. When you tell the truth and let the cards fall where they may, you will know the measure of true friendship. Does your friend understand? Does she forgive you? Hopefully she will. This is the mark of a true friend. And remember: one day the tables may turn and you will be in the position to forgive a friend who says no to you.

⁓ Common Courtesy ⁓

Common courtesies are the Manners 101 of the etiquette world. Sadly, it's a course that most of society is currently flunking. Common courtesy is saying "please" and "thank you." Saying "excuse me" when you bump into someone. Holding the door open for the person behind you. Common courtesy should govern the way you interact with everyone from the grocery checkout person to the janitor at your office. I include common courtesy in this chapter on communication because manners communicate respect to other people.

Because common courtesy is so rare nowadays, your manners will stand out like a rare gem to the person you are extending them to. How many times have you seen someone completely ignore the grocery clerk as the person chats on the phone? I'm sure this irks the grocery clerk to not be acknowledged. None of us are too busy or important to acknowledge with eye contact or a smile the people with whom we interact.

Common courtesies include the manners we were taught as children. Whenever I hear someone say, "Give me a cup of coffee," to a barista, I want to say, "What's the magic word?" "May I have a cup of coffee, please" is much more polite. When ordering at a restaurant, I used to say to the waiter, "I want." One day my husband (who knew!) said to me, "'I would like' is a much better way to phrase your request." Point taken. "I would like" does sound much more polite than "I want."

Have you ever let someone into your lane and not been thanked with a wave? If you're driving and trying to get into a lane, have you ever had someone speed up so you couldn't get in? When we practice common courtesy, we can change the climate of our neighborhood and in our small way inspire others to do so as well. Just a small wave of thanks to another driver might make that driver more likely to let others into his or her lane in the future. You never know what a small wave could mean.

Perhaps every morning you pass a neighbor on the sidewalk who ignores you. You could consistently say good morning to that neighbor each day with a cheerful smile. Don't worry if the neighbor responds to you or not. That is none of your business, and don't take offense if he or she doesn't. You are "keeping your side of the street clean" by greeting your neighbor. Sometimes when I encounter a grumpy neighbor who is intent on staring at the sidewalk intensely rather than greeting me, I shrink back and think I better not say hello. But this doesn't feel natural to me. It feels very unnatural to ignore my fellow man. So I always say hi. This usually brings the neighbor out of his or her funk, and that neighbor either says a belated hello or just looks at me in shock. Has life on earth become so impersonal that a simple greeting has become shocking? Perhaps.

As a poised person, practice common courtesy. Don't worry what others are doing or not doing in your vicinity. They will either come around or they won't. The point is to not compromise your integrity. Don't let other people get you down! Communicate your grace by employing common courtesy on a daily basis.

Punctuality

We try to be punctual. And we have the best intentions. But things happen. Traffic! Faulty directions! Children who don't want to wear shoes! Despite all of the forces working against us, poised people make punctuality a priority. Punctuality is a way of communicating respect for the people you are meeting. The best goal in any situation is to be early, with parties in private homes being the only exception (you do not want to show up to a party early and fluster the host!).

Here are five tips for poised punctuality:

1. Set a reminder for your appointment. **Many times people are late because they forgot they had to be somewhere in the first place! Most smartphones have a calendar with an alarm option. You can set it to remind you to be on time one hour or even one day before your event. It's helpful to write all pertinent information in your reminder, such as the address and notes on where to park. This way you have all the information you need in one space.**

2. Get everything ready beforehand. **If you have an early morning appointment, get everything in order the night before. Choose your clothes and lay them out. Pack that lunch and keep it in the fridge. Put your briefcase by the front door. Scout out the location and all potential routes.**

3. Leave room for the unexpected. **If you are traveling to a new location, the GPS might say it only**

takes you twenty minutes to get there, but that could be without traffic. Double the time you think it will take you to get there, in case you encounter a jam. If you think your children will be tough to rally, ask them to get ready ten minutes before you normally would, to account for any lagging.

4. Know the particulars. If you are driving, find out where you need to park. If you are taking public transit, calculate the routes beforehand. Then, if you happen to be running behind due to traffic or a late bus, you can eliminate further confusion upon arrival.

5. Be prepared to be early. If you arrive early, come prepared with a book or something to keep you occupied while you wait. Remember, being early is not a waste of time. It is simply ensuring that you don't arrive flustered and unprepared.

Email etiquette

When you first email someone, especially a business contact, you must follow formal email protocol. With friends or co-workers who frequently exchange emails with you, some of the formalities can be dropped, but it's always a great idea to keep common courtesy at the heart of your communication. Here are some things to consider:

Reply all? Before hitting "reply all" consider if you need to include everyone in this communication.

Forwarding? If you are forwarding an email, be sure to write a personal note before the forward. Never send chain emails.

Tone. Never write in all caps unless you want to give the impression that you are SHOUTING.

Mr. and Mrs. So and So. Don't let the casual nature of email put your guard down; always address your contact with the appropriate level of formality.

It's Jennifer with two n's. Make sure you spell everyone's name correctly.

Double-check. Don't forget to use spell-check if you've misspelled something.

Angry? Think before you hit send. Once an email is sent, it cannot be taken back.

Dot your i's and cross your t's. Use complete sentences rather than informal abbreviations or slang.

Sincerely, Employ polite common courtesies as you would in a letter. Start off with either "Dear" or "Hello." Inquire about the other person with a pleasantry such as "How are you?" or wish them well with "I hope this email finds you well." Don't forget to sign off gracefully just as you would at the end of a letter.

Returning calls and emails

We are bombarded with correspondence on a daily basis. With instant communication through text, phone, and email, people want a response and they want it now! For important calls and emails, the general rule is to try to respond within twenty-four hours. If you are busy and can't give a proper response to a call or an email within twenty-four hours, it is nice to respond by saying, "I have your message and will get back to you." Give a time frame for your response. If you are out of town or unable to return messages, you can set your email to send an automatic message saying you are unavailable to answer emails until you return. Do your best to get back to people upon your return. Do not feel the pressure to get back to lower-priority messages instantly; otherwise you will become a slave to text, phone, and email.

Screen time

We have all seen them. They are everywhere. You can't escape them. People staring at their smartphones like zombies. In restaurants, walking the dog, in the middle of a movie, while driving, waiting in line, in class, outside of class, during the ballet, during intermission, at the coffee shop, while watching TV, while out with their kids, at the park, at the school, during meetings. This new dependence on the screen is changing the way we live and not necessarily for the better.

The addiction to the screen and its use as a crutch in social situations brings people further away from poise. It brings them away from manners and social grace. I will take it a step further and suggest that it not only keeps us antisocial, but washes away whatever social graces we *used* to have. While on a walk recently I approached a young man standing on the sidewalk who was staring intently into his smartphone. As I approached, rather than look up at me, he turned his back on me as I walked near him and continued to text as he now faced the corner of the wall and a shrub. Really? Is this what we have become? Shunning real human connection in favor of a virtual life? As poised people, let's strive to not live life through our screens.

HELLO! I'M HERE!

Have you ever been out with a friend who will not stop checking his or her phone or texting someone else? You feel as though you are intruding on your friend's time, or that your friend is talking with someone who is more important than you. I'm not talking about the parent who keeps the phone out in case there is an emergency with the babysitter—we've all done that—I'm talking about people who have text conversations with other people on their phone while you're talking to them. If someone does this to you, resist the temptation to take out your phone and check your messages to make the other person (or yourself) feel better. Usually these people are oblivious to what they are doing. Just sit there and look at them while they giggle and text. Perhaps they will get the message? Depending on how comfortable you are with confrontation, you could also bring their behavior to the forefront. Or you could make a mental note not to go out with them again.

The text message trap

Before smartphones were invented, people had to ring the home phone, send an email, send a letter, or show up on your doorstep. Enter text message. All of that has changed. Texts are wonderful ways to stay in contact with people during the day. Many a dark day for me has been brightened by sharing a funny text conversation with a friend. But we do have to be aware of not becoming a slave to the text message alert. When you are engaged in something else and you hear the ding of your phone indicating you have a new text, do you drop everything and immediately check it out? Sometimes this is appropriate, but what about when we do this every time? People can contact us now wherever we are—whether at home or away—at all times of the day and night. What we have to remind ourselves as poised people is that we are not at their beck and call. People might expect you to get back to them immediately, but you do not need to feel that urgency. It can be very disruptive to the day if you constantly interrupt it to deal with messages from other people.

I have a rule that when I am spending quality time with my children, I do not pick up my phone. I don't care how many times my phone dings. I'll turn off the ringer and flip it over. I don't want my kids to see me constantly on my phone. When we are having a nice moment, reading a story or working on an art project, I don't want their hearts to fall heavy when they hear my phone, thinking that I will abandon our time together to go text my friends.

This is not something that has come easily to me. It can be exciting to get a text, but I have to use self-discipline during the day, when I am working and when I'm in the middle of family time, to not go there. Then in the evening, when I have downtime, I can text my friends with the day's updates to my heart's content.

It's a great idea to analyze how screen time has changed your life and how it alters your behavior. If you don't like what you see, implement changes. Get comfortable again with real human connection and don't give so much power to the screen and what is behind it. Real life is in the present moment, happening right now. We never know how many days we have in front of us. Let's live them fully, not virtually.

GOSSIP GIRL

Gossiping is a tempting vice. If you have something juicy on someone, you just want to get it off your chest! If someone has a scandalous bit of information about an acquaintance, you want to know what it is! But the poised person avoids gossip at all costs. Gossip is harmful. It is hurtful. All you have to do is put yourself in the shoes of the person being talked about. Would you want others to discuss you in this way? Never. That thought alone can stop it every time. You can say a word of defense for the other person, or you can merely walk away. If you can't step away, sometimes silence or a change of subject is the most powerful thing.

～ Public Speaking ～

Public speaking. Two words that strike fear in the heart of practically everyone on earth. Yet we all have to do it at some point in our lives. You might have to give a presentation at work. You are asked to give the maid-of-honor speech at a wedding. You are introducing the guest speaker at an event you organized at your child's school. You need to give your book report standing in front of the class. Ladies and gentlemen, public speaking can be scary. But it doesn't have to be, because you have a secret weapon, and that secret weapon is *poise*.

When I was in high school, I was tremendously shy. If the teacher asked me to read in front of the class, my voice would tremble violently. I'm not so sure what my problem was, but the thought of an entire room of people focusing their eyes on me and studying me was enough to make me want to go home and hide under my comforter for the rest of my life.

When I entered my senior year in high school, I knew something had to change. I couldn't go on like this, worrying what other people thought of me. Never one to shy away from my shortcomings, I decided to enroll in a drama class. Maybe standing on stage and delivering a memorized monologue in front of a group of my peers was just the tough medicine I needed to confront my fear of public speaking.

The first few weeks of drama class were rough. I continued to shake like a leaf each time I had to perform. I wondered what twisted and sadistic part of me had made the choice to submit myself to such ridicule week after week. Maybe public speaking just wasn't for me! Maybe I was meant to be a wallflower and not be in front of people after all. Thankfully my pride didn't allow me to quit. In fact, I decided to pump up the discomfort even more by auditioning for the school play. At my high school the play auditions were not in private. They were held in a multipurpose room, in front of the teachers, the director, tech people, and all of the students who were auditioning for the play. All in all there were about a hundred people in that room.

The play was Richard Brinsley Sheridan's *The Rivals*, and we were to read a monologue on stage. I waited patiently (and in mortal fear) for over an hour and a half as student after student took the stage to recite his or her chosen monologue—Lydia Languish for the girls and Captain Jack Absolute for the boys. As I watched, I gave myself a pep talk. The auditioners were certainly not rivaling Meryl Streep or Robert De Niro. Why on earth was I so self-conscious again? If they could get up there and monotonously recite a monologue, surely I could do that too, but with flair. My name was called. My heart started pounding heavily in my chest as I approached the stage. But as I stood on that stage in front of all of those people, something clicked.

I centered myself in the spotlight. I took a deep breath. I didn't allow anyone to rush me. I dismissed my negative thoughts. I dismissed them. And then, as though something came over me, I was transformed. I spoke loudly and clearly and, putting myself in Lydia's place, delivered that monologue with passion. My voice rang out like a bell and people took notice. Looking back, I think this must have been my first poised moment. I went home and told my parents that for the first time ever, I hadn't allowed my nervousness to get the better of me.

The next day at school, students were swarming around the casting announcement at the drama room. I pushed my way through the crowd and nearly fell over when I saw my name in the supporting role of Julia Melville. Fancy going from sheer terror of public speaking to having a supporting role in a school play! From that moment forward, I knew that I could conquer my public speaking phobia.

In public speaking, poise is your secret weapon. You must command the stage with your presence. Stand tall, with the authority of one who is meant to be there. You are the expert. You are the perfect person to deliver this talk. The minute a negative thought comes into your head to tell you you are not worthy, dismiss it entirely. You are completely worthy. Find your spotlight. Stand up straight. Take a deep breath. Speak loudly and clearly with conviction. Make eye contact if appropriate. Own the space with your body. Don't allow your body to stiffen up. Allow your hands and arms to flow gracefully as you talk. Use your entire body and don't just be a talking head. When you are finished, don't be cowed away. Stand there for a moment and soak in the glory of what you have just accomplished.

I've come a long way since that high school audition. Since then, I've spoken in front of audiences ranging from three thousand college students, to forty women in a private seminar, and virtually to people all around the world through my TEDx talk. Take it from me: poise is your key to successful public speaking.

5 tips for public speaking:
....

1. Own the space: Whether you are on stage or standing at the head of a table, get comfortable in the space as quickly as possible. Act as if you belong there (because you do!).

2. Good posture: All eyes will be on you. Your good posture is important now more than ever. Stand tall.

3. Project: Make sure everyone can hear what you're saying by speaking clearly and projecting your voice toward the back of the room. Rather than speaking from your throat, picture speaking from your belly. Let your words come out with strength and volume.

4. Don't be afraid to move: Avoid deer-caught-in-the-headlights syndrome by moving. It's okay to gesture with your hands and to walk around

(if appropriate). If you are being filmed, ask the director to define the parameters of your movement.

5. Make a connection: Whether you are pitching a job to potential clients or touting the merits of your best friend at her wedding, the entire point of public speaking is to make a connection with your audience. You have been asked to speak because you have something to impart that could benefit your viewers. Don't make the speech about you; make it about what you can give.

⁓ The Air of Mystery ⁓

The poised person is mysterious for many reasons. As we have already discussed, such people are rare and, therefore, intriguing. The way they act, the way they dress, the way they carry themselves is a mystery. How do they pull that off? How does that young mother handle her child having a tantrum in the grocery store so calmly? How does that woman make her clothes look so darn stylish? How does that lady handle conflicts at work with such a cool head?

When it comes to poise: less is more. This is especially true when it comes to poised communication. Maintain that air of mystery. What does this mean for us? It means that we don't unnecessarily share every aspect of our lives with mere acquaintances. We would not have a loud conversation in public that can be overheard by everyone. If we must take a phone call in a public space where others can hear us, we speak softly or try to walk away so as not to disturb others.

We also guard what we post online. We don't need to jump on Facebook and update our status for every triumph, milestone, mundane thing, complaint, or whimsy. We don't need to share a close-up of our broken toe, for example. When we post about other people, we are sensitive. We don't need to post endless pictures of our children. We keep their wishes in mind. When they are older, will they want thousands of pictures of themselves online? We are empathetic. We put ourselves in other people's shoes. How would we feel if someone was posting pictures of us online that we had no say over? It would feel like a violation. We keep these things sacred. We keep them private. We have fun on social media and share with our close friends, but we don't need to share the intimate details of everyday life with hundreds of people we hardly know.

Cultivating an air of mystery can also be practiced in conversation. We all say things that are better left unsaid. You might be dishing with an acquaintance, saying negative things about your spouses. Or you might find yourself in the company of work colleagues who only like to bad mouth the boss behind the boss's back. You might feel tempted to join in and vent. Venting is certainly appropriate when you pick the right person to speak to. But do make sure that you are discussing these sensitive subjects with the right person and that you aren't just rehashing your problems with everyone you meet.

Poise resides in the space between our thoughts. If we pause, we are less likely to say something that is not in our best interest. We will not engage in a "Twitter feud" because we will have paused and assessed. Your secrets will stay safe. We must remember that poise is in the pause. Pausing when agitated. Pausing when excited. Pausing before saying something that isn't wise to say.

Part 3

PRACTICING POISE

Chapter 7

GRACIOUS WITH GUESTS

It is very easy to get flustered when you are having people over. You start to worry about everything from how you look to how clean your house is to whether or not they'll like the food. The funny thing is, these things fall very low on the priority list of what your guests really care about. Of course it's important to present yourself well. You wouldn't want to open the door in sloppy sweats or have your house look like a complete clutter-war zone, and naturally you want the food to please, but what your guests are really looking forward to when they visit you is . . . *you*! Good friends just want to see your face. They want to relax. They want to laugh. They want to catch up on news. They want to escape their own lives for a little while and enjoy your company. It's *you* they want. They don't want a stressed-out version of you because you're worried your baseboards are dusty. They don't want you to not listen to their story because you're worried that you're having a bad hair day. They don't want you constantly apologizing for the dish you made. They are just happy you made it!

Madame Chic was the epitome of the poised hostess. She was gracious and welcoming. As soon as her guests walked through the door, Madame Chic took their coats and bags and placed them in a designated area. Drinks were offered immediately. We would all enjoy our aperitif (my favorite part of her dinner parties!) in the living room along with lively discussions, our healthy appetites anticipating the dinner ahead.

When she ushered us into the dining room, she showed each of us where she had planned for us to sit. The female guest of honor was served first, followed by the rest of the women, and then the men were served. Every action was planned and was dignified, yet not stuffy at all. Madame Chic knew what to do, so we knew what to do. She made everyone feel comfortable. Conversations continued to be interesting and lively right through the courses until the end with dessert and coffee or a digestif. Music was enjoyed in the living room after dinner, and the whole affair went over as smoothly as a delicious glass of port. Madame Chic never apologized for her house, her appearance, or her food. She accepted guests with confidence and warmth, only wanting to provide a memorable experience for them.

A poised person's ease and confidence in social situations puts others at ease. As a guest, you know what to expect. When you walk into her home, you know you are going to be greeted and taken care of. It can be intimidating to walk into a cocktail party or a dinner party. The poised hostess puts her guests first and sees the event from the guest's point of view. This requires planning and preparation. When someone comes into your home, you should be there to greet that person, and if you're not able to do that, you should have someone else act as the official greeter (your children or husband, for example). I once walked into a party where I didn't see the hostess for nearly thirty minutes because she was busy mixing drinks and taking care of behind-the-scenes business. This might have been fine if I'd known her well or known other guests at the party, but I didn't know anyone. I just introduced myself to the other guests, but it would have been nice if the hostess or someone else had been there to welcome the people who walked in and were milling around her living room. No matter how busy you are, you must put in extra effort to greet guests who are new to the group and don't know others.

As Madame Chic would, show your guests where to place their bags and coats (or take care of those items for them) and offer them something to drink. If they don't know anyone else at the party, introduce them to another guest before you leave them. Make every guest feel like the "guest of honor."

When you are talking to your guests, give them your full attention. Don't look over their shoulder to see who else you can talk to or to see what's going on at the other end of the room. This can be tricky when you are speaking to someone who won't stop talking. If this is the case, and you feel that you are neglecting your hostess duties by talking to this person for too long, just interject an "excuse me" during a break in the conversation. Then try to introduce that person to someone else before you leave.

If you're having only one or two people over, it is significantly easier to receive them well. Make them feel warm and welcomed even if they show up early and take you by surprise. Remember, things don't have to be perfect to have friends over. They just want to see you. Welcome them, invite them in, and show them where to place their belongings. The rest is easy! Sit in armchairs by the fire with a cup of tea or sit out in the garden with an iced drink. Unless you need to have your phone out for emergency purposes, put it away and don't check it every few minutes. Give your guests your full attention.

HOSPITALITY CHALLENGE

Invite a neighbor over for tea this week! If you haven't received someone in your home in a while, this can be scary. We can be so insulated in our own lives that it can be intimidating to have someone in our private space. Take the plunge and extend the invitation to your neighbor. In a gentler time this practice was much more commonplace. These days our neighbors never see the inside of our homes and we never see theirs. But we are in our community together. It's a great way to strengthen bonds and friendships. Your gathering need not be fancy. A simple cup of tea and some cookies (homemade or store-bought) are perfectly acceptable. Your neighbor will be so charmed. It might be the first time she has ever been asked to tea! If you enjoy it, you can make it a regular thing. Slowing down for one afternoon and spending your time with a neighbor can be a reinvigorating experience and is a wonderful way for you to practice your poise.

⤳ Feeding Your Guests ⤵

The poised hostess keeps her guests' basic needs in mind first. There are a few rules of thumb when providing food for your guests. If people have traveled far to see you, you should offer them food and drink or, at the very least, a snack and a drink when they arrive. Let's say your guests just arrived from the airport, or have driven over an hour to come see you: give them water and ask if they'd like anything else to drink (coffee, hot tea, soda, iced tea). When it is not a mealtime, I put out a small plate of snacks, either tea biscuits or fruit or a bowl of nuts for them to nibble on. I never ask if they want these snacks because often people are too polite and don't want you to go to any trouble for them. If they aren't hungry and don't eat anything, that's just fine; it's the gesture that counts, and more often than not, you'll find that they are very grateful for your offering.

Another rule of thumb to remember is: don't invite people over during a mealtime unless you intend to provide a meal. I have often left playdates at people's houses during lunchtime feeling queasy with hunger pains because food was served to the kids but not to the adults. I understand that it can be intimidating to provide a meal for several adults and kids, and if this is the case for you, invite them over at 2 p.m. and offer crackers, juice, and grapes! Less pressure.

> Use your best
> The beautiful rests on the foundations
> of the necessary.
> —Ralph Waldo Emerson

We're living in a casual time, when the gravity of hostess duties seems irrelevant or outdated. Therefore, it's important that those of us who care, who are committed to cultivating poise, don't let the climate of our current culture dictate how we receive people in our home. Don't feel silly for using your best plates, teacups, and cloth napkins when you invite a neighbor over for a cup of tea and a brownie. Your guest probably won't be used to being treated so grandly and will most likely act surprised. Don't let self-consciousness get the better of you and start apologizing for things in a self-deprecating way. Just simply be your poised self with conviction and graciousness. You might inspire her to dust off her china and use her best things on a regular basis too. One thing is for certain, you will make your guest feel very special, and she will know what she means to you. If you don't have any "nice" dishes, don't worry! Entertaining is not about showing off your expensive possessions, it's about welcoming your guests, making them feel special, and spending time with them. You can do that even if every plate you own is old and chipped. It's the warm and confident way in which you act—your best self—that will win them over.

⌒ The Poised Guest ⌒

It is much easier to be a guest than to be a hostess, as there are fewer logistics to consider, but it is still worth looking at what makes a poised guest. Miss Bunting, the outspoken schoolteacher from season five of *Downton Abbey*, was a notoriously bad guest. She regularly challenged and insulted her host, Lord Grantham, at the dinner table, causing many a toe-curling, cringe-worthy moment. While a bad guest might make for good TV, it's never a good idea to be this person in real life.

Here are a few things to consider as a guest:

Always arrive with an offering appropriate for the occasion. It could be a basket of lemons from your backyard, a bottle of wine, some homemade cookies, a box of chocolates. When someone invites you into their home, bringing an offering is a great way to show your gratitude.

Avoid arriving early. (But don't be too late.)

Avoid staying too late. Be mindful of when the party is scheduled to end and plan on leaving by that time.

Don't monopolize too much of your host's time. Allow

your host to circulate the room to check on the other guests.

Never insult your host (ahem, Miss Bunting).

If conversation gets heated at the party, avoid fanning the flames by contributing incendiary comments. Remember everyone is entitled to an opinion. If someone's opinion differs from yours, that person is allowed to speak his or her mind. If tensions get high, consider changing the subject or observing the humor in the situation.

~ The Overnight Guest ~

I have a lot to say about being an overnight guest in someone else's home, as that was essentially what I was for the semester I lived with *Famille Chic*. It was clear upon entering their house that they did things a "certain way," and I made it my job to figure out that way and fit in as nicely as possible. Theirs was not a casual, "anything goes" house. I never would have left any of my belongings in their living room, for example. I kept all of my things in my bedroom. I also kept my bedroom as tidy as possible. The rest of the house was extremely tidy, so I wasn't about to let my room be the messy room. Plus, I don't think Madame Chic would have tolerated that! I was very respectful of mealtimes, and I never even went to the kitchen for so much as a snack, as that would have disrupted dinner plans. I went with the rhythm of the house.

The Chics only had one bathroom. One of the first questions Madame Chic asked me after settling me in was if I took morning or evening baths. Hmmm. I had never quite thought about that before. I guess I took both! I liked a bath every morning and sometimes before bed too. My wishy-washy answer was met with a look of consternation from Madame Chic. It was clear that *that* wouldn't be happening. She continued to stare at me as I fine-tuned my answer. "Mornings, please," I said sheepishly. So mornings it was. Because the whole family had to use the same bathroom, there had to be a set schedule in place. They did this to avoid any traffic jams for someone needing to get ready for work but having to wait for the person lounging in an impromptu bubble bath.

Don't forget when you do use the bathroom to lock the door! Oh yes, you know what I am about to say. On the second day of my stay, I was using the bathroom, and lo and behold, Monsieur Chic walked right in on me. *POURQUOI* had I not locked the door? So embarrassing. M. Chic was a gentleman about it of course, but what a way to start my stay.

When you travel, whether it is to visit your parents in your childhood home or to a grand hotel, take note of how you "live" outside of your home. Don't let your good practices drop here. Upon arriving at your destination, check to see if there is a place for you to store your clothes: a closet with free hangers or a few empty drawers are all that is needed. Neatly put away your clothes and then store your suitcase out of sight if possible. Even if there is maid service, such as in a hotel, be sure not to "trash" your room, and be conscious about how you keep your belongings. If you are staying at a friend or family member's home, be sure that you make your bed and keep your room tidy. If you must live out of your suitcase, keep your clothes packed as neatly as you can. We are taking the great practice that we have established at home and using it abroad.

Once, when I was traveling with a girlfriend for work, she came into my hotel room and joked that I made my bed even when there was maid service. I do because I can't stand an unmade bed! I can't think in a room where the bed is rumpled. On the flip side, however, I recently noticed that when I return to visit my parents, I let my room become a disaster! It's as if my old room brings out the messy teenager in me. When my daughters walked into my room one day, I noticed how my clothes were scattered around the suitcase, chair, and bed and my other belongings were littered all over the room. I didn't want them to see me living like that, and now I make an extra effort to be tidy when visiting my parents.

How to be a good overnight guest:

Always bring your hosts a gift.
Never leave your belongings in the common areas;
try to keep them in your room.
Keep your room as tidy as possible.

Always clean up after yourself, especially in the
bathroom and kitchen.

Be respectful of the house rules.

Be mindful of mealtimes.

Lock the bathroom door.

Make sure you are not hogging the shared
bathroom.

Don't have phone conversations in front of your
hosts; always excuse yourself before making or
answering a phone call.

Avoid excess texting or looking at your phone when
with your hosts.

If you are staying for an extended stay, be sure to
give your hosts some time off. Take off for an
afternoon by yourself. Don't expect them to
entertain you the entire time.

Offer to make or buy them dinner at least one of the
nights you are there.

Leave a parting gift or thank-you note for them.

Strip the bed of the sheets on your last morning
there.

A poised hostess knows that her welcoming warmth will make her guests feel comfortable and at home. She invites guests over regularly to entertain. Her home is a place full of life, where people want to be. So whether you are a hostess or a guest, enjoy meaningful connection with your friends on a regular basis and let these experiences enrich your life.

Chapter 8

DARLING AT DINNER

I don't know about you, but when mealtime is chaotic I get indigestion. Peace, tranquillity, and good table manners are all we ask for to enjoy a simple meal, right? So why is it so hard to achieve this on a Wednesday evening? In an ideal world, once mealtime begins, all other outside activities not pertaining to dining should cease. If you are eating by yourself, a peaceful mealtime is quite easy to achieve. No distractions, no screens, everything set before you, no getting up or wiping faces (other than your own, of course). But eating with your family? That's an entirely different pétanque game. Family members might come and go as they please from the table. You might find yourself getting up every few minutes to get things for your children. Cups of grape juice will be tipped over by accident on the white tablecloth. Ketchup will be smeared on a place mat. Your husband will burp. This isn't quite the elegant meal you'd hoped for.

Jamais peur! Because luckily, cultivating poise at the dinner table starts with *you* and you alone. If you are in a season of life where your young children view the dining table as a playground, just continue to give them loving guidance on what we do at the table and remember that this phase won't last forever. When I see my toddler teetering off her chair as she eats her peas via her fists, I remind myself that she won't be doing this at twenty-four (one hopes!).

Delight in the challenge of being the light of elegance in an otherwise dark quagmire of bad table manners. When you take your seat, sit tall (remember that good posture!), lay your cloth napkin in your lap, and enjoy your meal. Don't be in a rush to eat even though everyone around you is wolfing down food. Corrections to children should be gracious. Avoid scolding or constant directions. We want our children to enjoy good table manners. Make it look fun and enticing.

When we prepare a meal, lay down the tablecloth, pour

the drinks, and carefully place the silverware and plates, we are upholding tradition: the marvelous gift we get to have each day of breaking bread with one another. As we lay the table, we also lay the foundation to nourish, recharge, and connect. We nourish our bodies with the food we eat. This is why peace and focus at the table are so critical. If we are eating dinner while scrolling Instagram on our iPhone, we have no connection with what is being eaten.

Let's treasure our dining traditions. Let's not eat in front of the TV or alone in our bedroom. Let's spend time with one another and connect again over food. Let's revive old traditions such as giving toasts, giving thanks, and waiting until everyone is finished eating before getting up. Let's share how our day went. Let's thank the cook for dinner! Let's help clean up. Let's all sit up tall and enjoy this meal, even if it is just pizza (again!). And remember, if these things are important to you, but seemingly not important to those you are eating with, carry on. Be the catalyst for reviving the poised dinner.

HOW-TO: EATING DIFFICULT FOODS

To avoid any awkward reenactments of the escargot scene from *Pretty Woman*, make sure you are well versed on how to eat difficult foods.

Artichokes: With your hand, remove one leaf at a time and dip into the accompanying sauce. Place the soft end in your mouth and pull through your teeth. Discard the rest by placing it on the plate provided.

Asparagus: If the asparagus is firm and unsauced, you may pick up the hard end with your fingers to eat. If there is a sauce, you eat it with a knife and fork. When in doubt, always use utensils.

Cherry tomatoes: When eating these as an hors d'oeuvres, always pop the entire cherry tomato into your mouth. Never bite it in half, as it will most likely squirt your companion in the face (not chic). When they are eaten in a salad, cut whole cherry tomatoes carefully and with little pressure using a knife and fork.

Escargot: Slippery suckers, those. With one hand, grip the shell with seafood tongs, and then pull out the meat with the seafood fork provided. Dip the meat in the accompanying sauce.

Lobster or crab: Use a nutcracker to crack the shell then extract the meat with the seafood fork provided. Now dip the meat in the accompanying sauce and enjoy! You may suck the meat out of the small claws, but avoid making any loud suction noises when doing this.

Oysters: If desired, squeeze lemon juice on your oyster. Detach the oyster from its shell by gently rolling the provided seafood fork underneath the meat. Add any desired sauce, such as mignonette or cocktail sauce. Then pick up the oyster and allow it to slowly slide into your mouth. Don't inhale while you do this, as you could suck the oyster down your throat. (I've seen this happen before, it's not pretty.)

Spaghetti: Twirl a few strands (the key word being "few") on your fork and then eat. You never want to get a giant ball of pasta going on your fork because then you will either be obligated to eat it, or you will have to start all over again. If you wish, you may use a spoon to twirl the pasta against.

⌇ Faux Pas at the Table ⌇

Madame Chic was usually very tactful when she corrected my behavior in her home. So tactful, in fact, that after the correction took place, I wondered what had just happened. I was normally very receptive to her tutelage, although near the end of my stay, she gave me some etiquette advice at the dinner table that did not go over so well . . .

It was *Famille Chic*'s custom to have a baguette with every dinner (actually every breakfast too, and if you want to get technical, probably every lunch). When they offered the cheese course at the end of the dinner, they passed around the cheese plate, starting with me, as I was the female guest of honor. I then would select a slice of cheese (usually Camembert, my favorite) and then pass the plate back to Madame

Chic, who would serve herself. The custom of the cheese tray is not one that we know much about in America, and during my entire stay with the Chics, I would spread the cheese on my entire piece of bread and then take a bite of the bread. In doing this, I basically committed one of the biggest *fromage* faux pas one can commit. I'm sure Madame Chic looked on with silent horror each evening as I spread the cheese on the entire piece of bread and chomped down. But she suffered this indelicacy in silence for the first five months I lived with them. Perhaps she was feeling bold this evening, or perhaps she thought she just couldn't send me back to America with this unsavory habit without at least attempting to school me on it first. With sensitivity, trying not to humiliate me, she explained to me that in France (in case I hadn't noticed over the past five months!), they rip off a small piece of bread, spread a small piece of cheese on the bread, then place the tasty prepared morsel into their mouths, only to repeat the process until both bread and cheese are gone. I must have been having a bad day, because I then said to Madame Chic, "I'm sorry, but there are just so many rules to remember. What does it matter how I eat my cheese as long as I enjoy it?"

It was the Miss Bunting moment of my trip in Paris. An awkward silence ensued. Madame Chic apologized and went on with her cheese course. The men at the table turned bright red. Hmmm. I definitely could have handled *that* better! The thing is we get defensive when we are corrected. We like to think we do things the right way and that we do no wrong. My ego was too big to take in the horror that I had been eating cheese incorrectly for five months. If I could relive that moment again, I would say "*Merci*" (even if I *was* annoyed) and try the cheese her way. So if you find that you are committing a faux pas in a new culture, don't jump to defend yourself, but try it their way. Who knows, you might like their way and, as I did, find out you don't know everything after all!

SCREENS IN RESTAURANTS

Parents, I know. You never get to have a civilized dinner anymore. You can't see any end in sight of your children, wiggling, spilling, whining, and getting silly at the supper table. All you want is one night of peace.

You take them to a restaurant and they start to act up. It can be so tempting to get out your phone or the iPad so they will just sit still and watch a show. But I urge you not to do this. Children have to learn eventually to sit at a table and engage with other people without being visually stimulated. They need to learn poise at the table. Persevere, no matter how annoying it is, in teaching your kids the value of sitting at a table and eating with the family. Don't let them become little screen zombies at the restaurant so you can get a break. Don't worry, they won't do this forever, and as soon as you know it you'll be taking your bright young son or daughter out to lunch and laughing about when he or she used to wiggle and crawl under the table to tickle your feet.

⌒ Faux Pas at the Bar ⌒

During social gatherings practice restraint with alcohol. You know your level of tolerance, and it is never advisable to go over that. Never drink and drive. And remember buzzed driving is drunk driving. Poised people know their limits. For me, one glass of wine at a social dinner is completely sufficient. Two would be my absolute maximum. I have had dinners with people who have had more than seven alcoholic drinks—and that was just during the meal! Poised people do not need to get drunk to have a good time. If you feel that you have a problem with drinking, get real with yourself. Addiction to alcohol is a serious problem. Seek help by joining a 12-step program or other supportive community. As for drugs? There is only one rule in my book: just say *non*!

HOW-TO: WINE SAMPLING

When sampling wine at a restaurant, remember three steps: look, smell, and taste:

1. Look: Have a look at the wine in the glass to approve of its color. White wines should be crisp and clear, for example, not cloudy. Red wines should be rich and pure in color, and a rosé will have a pink or blush tint.
2. Smell: Swirl the wine in your glass and inhale its scent deeply. Smelling is really the first tasting, as the aroma the wine emits will foretell what's to come. What notes do you detect? Keep this in mind as you taste.
3. Taste: Now take a sip and swirl it around in your mouth, taking note of its characteristics. Sweet? Bitter? Robust? Are the characteristics in line with the notes you smelled? Are the flavors balanced and in harmony? If so, proceed with the pouring and enjoy.

Dining need not be a stressful experience. Breaking bread with people is one of the true joys in life. When you practice good table etiquette on a daily basis, whether you are lunching alone at home or dining with friends in a fancy restaurant, remember that the most important thing is to savor your food and, if you are in the company of others, bond over life. Poised people enjoy themselves during meals and understand the wisdom that there is dignity in dining well.

Chapter 9

CHEZ VOUS AND BEYOND

You will travel to many places in your life, but every journey will start from home. Get your home life in order and everything else can follow suit. As poised people it is important that we take our poise with us wherever we are, whether we are behind closed doors or in crowds of people. We are making our poise a way of life. Let's explore how we can be poised *chez nous* and beyond.

An Ordered Home

An ordered home makes room for poise. Chaos, disorder, and clutter stress us out. They are the symptoms of mayhem and pandemonium. Remember our home life, our life behind closed doors, is where we practice cultivating poise. It is where we lay the foundation and set the precedent for how we act in the outside world. Committing to bringing your home to order is an exercise in self-discipline. Self-discipline builds character, and good character leads to poise.

Much as with our clothes, we can tend to hold on to belongings in our home that are past their prime, that don't fit in with our other belongings, or that we just don't even love. My husband likes to call these things "tat." "Tat" describes a tasteless article in a tatty condition. That owl lamp you got as a gift when you were in college. That broken green fruit bowl you just can't seem to get rid of. That rickety old trunk you picked up at a garage sale. The dead orchid plants around your house. That picture frame that doesn't quite fit in. There is tremendous freedom in getting rid of all of these things. Throw them away if they are broken or give them away to someone who could make better use of them. Make sure everything that you keep in your home is in top shape, contributes to the overall style of your home, and is of use. It is better to live with minimal furniture than to have an over-abundance of stuff that makes your home feel chaotic. Go through each room and be honest about what you need to get rid of. That old high chair that your toddler doesn't use any-more, that solo candlestick that hasn't seen its mate in over a year, that ugly alarm clock that gives you bad vibes every time you look at it—they can all go. You will start this process with trepidation. It will initially be hard for you to get rid of that funny vase you never use and don't even really like. But then, as you get rid of things, you'll start to feel giddy. You can do this! You'll gather a momentum and see how great your room looks when it is clear of unnecessary tat.

Yes, clutter, order, and poise are all related to one another. When you clear your home of clutter, you create a healthy foundation to live out your poise. If your living room is choked by disordered belongings, you subconsciously act and dress accordingly. You might skip the presentable pajamas and wear frumpy sweats because, who cares? Your posture will slump because you feel defeated. The seeming mountain of work that needs to be done is too monstrous, so what's the point of even trying to better yourself in this mess? You might feel like a sham. Who are you trying to fool cultivating poise amid the utter chaos of your home?

Here's the encouraging news. You can cultivate poise no matter where you are or what the circumstances. Let's say you live with a messy roommate. How she lives is completely out of your control, and just because she lives that way doesn't mean you might as well forget living a poised life. Maybe you are a mother of three, and you start to feel discouraged with all of the toy cars, space machines, and dollies scattered around the house. What's the point of poise when you are constantly fighting muddy footprints and mountains of toys? As we will discuss later in the book, difficult situations are the most important times to employ poise.

Time commitment

We are looking at two types of time commitments to keep our home in order. The first is a longer, initial commitment that might take a weekend or two of getting rid of major and minor items in the home, clearing the way to establish our routines. The second time commitment comes from the everyday, small decisions we make to keep our home in order. This commitment never ceases. Even if you are living with a family who have messy tendencies and who do not value order as much as you do, keep persevering. Don't let them get you down! If you have children, your orderly ways will rub off on them. The disciplined way you live will leave an impression on them. Establish routines for all areas of your life that are lacking order. Set the incoming mail and filing in the same place every time, for example. Commit to put away the breakfast things right after breakfast rather than leaving them for later in the day. Make sure the clothes actually fall into the dirty clothes hamper instead of keeping them strewn on the floor or the racks in the bathroom. Concentrating on these routines may slow you down at first, but ultimately they will bring you to a place of clearer consciousness.

Even if you didn't have a good role model to show you how to be neat and tidy when you were growing up, it's never too late to learn and change. You can fight the bad habits you picked up and commit to living a clear, ordered, and beautiful life. Begin to analyze how you keep everything in your home, from your makeup to your hair tools. Are they just heaped in a drawer in a chaotic jumble? Or is there order and method to how they are stored? When you pull out your hair dryer, do the flat iron, curling iron, and two types of hairbrushes spill out onto the floor? If this is a problem for you, be sure to look at what you are storing. Chances are you are storing a lot of things you never use and don't need. This is particularly apparent in bathroom cabinets. We will hold on to bottles with hardly any product in them, free samples, and old dusty candles. They must all go. If you never or rarely use it, seriously consider getting rid of it.

⁓ How to Be a Good Neighbor ⁓

A good neighbor is a fellow who
smiles at you over the back fence, but
doesn't climb over it.

—Arthur Baer

We all want to live in a nice neighborhood. We all want to live next to "good" neighbors. This starts with us. If we are mindful of being the best neighbors we can be, we elevate the quality of our neighborhood and could inspire others to do the same. Here are some tips on how to be a good neighbor:

Keep the front of your home tidy. Whether you rent or own, never let your front yard fall into disrepair. One of my favorite television shows of all time is *Keeping Up Appearances*. I always laughed at how horrified Hyacinth Bucket was when she visited her sister Daisy's house, because Daisy's front yard was such a trip with its run-down old car, broken fence, and bottles strewn everywhere. While that is quite funny on television, I would not be amused to live next to such a home. If you have a garden, arrange to keep the landscaping tidy. If you only have a front porch or even just an apartment door, do not leave miscellaneous items outside. Sweep your front step often. Dispose of all trash as soon as possible.

Be aware of noise. If you are going to have a raucous party, it's a good idea to tell your neighbors about it beforehand so they know what to expect. Don't let the party go into the wee hours of the morning, and try to end it at a fairly decent hour. You don't want the cops to shut you down. If you live in a home with shared walls, try not to play loud music during sleeping hours. If you have neighbors below you, try not to walk too loudly or let your children jump incessantly.

Be mindful of your lighting. If you have any outside spotlights, be sure that they are not illuminating your neighbor's boudoir at midnight.

Don't let your dog bark incessantly. If you know you have a yapper (Gatsby, I'm looking at you), while you are away don't leave your dog outside, where he or she will disrupt the entire neighborhood.

Discuss problems in person. If there are any problems, the best way to broach them is to talk to your neighbor in person. My next-door neighbor in Santa Monica used to turn her study light on at 2 a.m. This light would flood through the windows into my bedroom and wake me up. I thought about getting black-out shades, but then when I saw her walking her dog, I simply asked if she could tilt her shutters up rather than down. She was more than happy to do so and apologized. I thanked her for being so accommodating. It was handled right away.

Get to know your neighbors. If new neighbors move in, bake them some cookies or bring them a basket of fruit from your tree to welcome them into the neighborhood. Get to know your neighbors and be friendly with them. Say hello and invite them over for a cup of tea every now and then. When you are friendly with your neighbors, it creates an atmosphere of peace in the neighborhood and builds community bonds.

NOT JUST THE HOME

Celebrity party planner Colin Cowie wrote in his book *Chic* that when interviewing candidates to work for him, he often would look at the state of their purse (from afar, of course!) or walk them to their car to stealthily peer inside. He could tell a lot about the candidate by how the person kept his or her personal space. If the car was littered with fast-food wrappers, cigarette ashes, old socks, and paperwork, that indicated a lack of care for one's belongings. Keeping all of your spaces tidy is an extended representative of your poise.

⟿ Poise at Work ⟿

Employing poise at work is crucial. Potential advancements, promotions, customers, and clients are all dependent on you! (No pressure.) No matter what business you work in, whether you are the head honcho or you're sifting letters in the mailroom, poise is your greatest asset at work. It will get you noticed and you, my friend, will go far because of it. There is much to remember but no need to be overwhelmed. Here are a few reminders:

Always act with integrity and dignity. Honesty is one of the most important traits you can have at work. Your coworkers, clients, and customers need to feel that they can trust you and are in good hands. Always be truthful whether you are clocking in your hours or listing your accomplishments in the interview.

First impressions are important. Whether it's a new client or a new district manager, always stand when you're being introduced to someone. Exchange a good, solid handshake (never *faire la bise*!) with good eye contact and a friendly smile.

Be a good listener. Let's say you are receiving a performance review from your boss and he or she gives you a few areas you could improve upon. This hurts your pride. You might feel defensive, annoyed, and even upset. But it's a good idea to place your pride on the back burner and genuinely listen to your boss's analysis. Get truthful with yourself. Are any of your boss's points valid? Show your boss you are truly listening and are interested in improving yourself. Clients and customers need to feel heard. Coworkers need to feel heard. Your boss needs to be heard. Being a good listener at work shows you are a team player. In return you will be respected and people will listen to your points.

Look alert. I know you're tired and this Monday-morning meeting is such a complete and total drag, but perk up, sit straight, and look alert. You can raise the energy level and productivity of your team. Your enthusiasm will be infectious. True leaders are enthusiastic and energetic, not lethargic.

Always dress appropriately. It is best to err on the side of conservative dress. Never wear clothing that is too revealing, either too short or showing too much cleavage. Dress for the job that you want, not the job that you have. Aim to look presentable always. First impressions matter, and people make judgments based on the first few seconds of seeing you, before you've even spoken. Make sure you are representing yourself in a way that is visually appropriate.

No visible tattoos or body piercings. If you work in a conservative environment, it is best to cover them up. Whether you like it or not, people will judge you for them, and you do not want them to hinder your chances of getting the job, promotion, or new account.

Treat everyone with kindness and courtesy, from the janitor to the CEO. Do this not to get ahead, but to show respect for everyone in the workplace. Treating everyone with equal reverence creates a positive team environment. Everyone there contributes in his or her own special way and everyone is important.

Be diplomatic in how you communicate. Avoid pointing, as it looks aggressive. If you must point, keep two fingers together. Think politician. Also think (and pause) before you speak. If you work in human resources or customer service, you might deal with many irate people. Maintain your calm and poise even in the wake of their angry tirades. You are the face of the company. Bite your tongue if you feel like snapping back. If you're refereeing a back-and-forth between two coworkers, be diplomatic and let each person know that his or her side has been heard. Be the calm in the middle of the storm.

Watch your language. It doesn't matter how friendly you are with your coworkers, watch your language lest the boss or, even worse, a customer, hears you swear. I once heard an airline steward drop the f-bomb. It was shocking for me and embarrassing for him.

Show respect for the common areas like the kitchen or tea area. Clean up after yourself. Never take any food that isn't yours. Avoid taking personal calls in these areas, so as not to disturb others who are resting.

Keep your work area tidy. Doing so showcases a good work ethic and shows you respect the job. Treat your work space as you would the big corner office with the view, even if you are just in a cubicle for now.

Always be punctual for meetings. You do not want to step into that boardroom with twelve sets of annoyed glances looking your way.

Never gossip. If others are participating in office gossip, stand up for the person being gossiped by pointing out that that person is not there to defend him- or herself, or simply remove yourself from the situation.

Take responsibility if you have acted in error. It shows tremendous courage to own up to your mistakes. Stepping up with integrity will most likely erase much of the damage done by the mistake in the first place.

Don't order extravagantly at business dinners. I know the lobster looks good and so does that bottle of champagne, but employ restraint when ordering at business meals, to show respect for the hosts.

Never order a take-away bag from a business dinner. It just looks bad. And then you have to carry it out of the restaurant. Awkward.

Be yourself. From the initial interview to every day thereafter, strive to be yourself. There's a reason you got this job in the first place. They like you and you are a great fit! Even if this is not your dream job, give it your best effort and wow them with your poise. Who knows where it will lead?

⤳ Dating and Poise ⤳

Single poised ladies, I have some wonderful news for you: as you work on polishing your poise, you are more likely to attract a man who values the same things in life. When you dress beautifully, behave graciously, and exude class wherever you go, people will notice. You will be intriguing to those who also care about these things. With your excellent manners and grace you will automatically weed out all of the potential suitors who are, well, not suitable. Most women want a kind-hearted man with honesty and integrity who will treat them well. We want a partner to go through life with who shares our values and is on the "same page" as us.

It is said that when two people are dating they are presenting their best selves. Often after the honeymoon phase is over, one's "true self" comes out. Well, when you are in the dating phase, you will be presenting your "true self," because your true self will be the lovely, poised, elegant person you are! I am not a dating expert, but I did marry a pretty amazing man and have been happily married now for nearly a decade. Here are my thoughts on dating with poise:

Always present your authentic self. Never hide things or pretend to be someone you are not in order to impress a man.

Dress alluringly, yet tastefully. You should feel both comfortable and stylish in your clothes. You want him to focus on you, not your cleavage, so don't feel the need to lure him that way. Your intelligence and natural beauty is enough!

Discuss interesting things such as your favorite books, films, and places to travel. Get an idea of what common interests you share.

Never feel pressured to do anything you are not comfortable with.

If he insists on paying, accept graciously, but be sure to treat him to something down the line, whether it's lunch the next week or a meal you make for him.

On the first date maintain your air of mystery. He doesn't

need to know your entire dating history or why the last guy jilted you. These things can come out later, but for the first date, keep it light.

I know first dates can be nerve-racking, but don't get drunk! Keep your wits about you and never go over the limit of how much alcohol you can tolerate.

Avoid expressing your emotions online or in texts. Be respectful of what you share about your new beau on social media.

Take your time. Just as you'd savor a delicious feast, savor the romance and how it unfolds. Don't rush things. This is the most magical time in the relationship!

If you really like him, let him know. There is no need to play silly games. Remember, you are a catch! He will most likely be thrilled to have snagged such a poised lady.

TIPPING WITH CONFIDENCE

In America, the standard tip to be left at a restaurant is 15 to 20 percent of the cost of the bill. I always leave 20 percent (those waiters need our tips!). Plus, it's easier for me to calculate the math for 20 percent rather than 15 percent. Many restaurants will calculate the projected tip for you, but if they don't, there is no need for you to stress out. If you're dubious of your head math, you can always bring out the calculator on your phone (just try to be discreet about it and don't check your email afterward). Use this list as a guideline to help you navigate the modern guidelines for tipping in various circumstances.

TIPPING CHART:

Waiter/waitress: 15 percent of bill for regular service, 20 percent for excellent service

Sommelier: 15 percent cost of the bottle

Bartender: 15 to 20 percent of the tab or, at a minimum, $1 per alcoholic beverage

Food delivery: 10 percent of bill

Coatroom attendant: $1 per coat

Valet: $2 to bring your car to you

Washroom attendant: $1

Taxi driver: 15 to 20 percent

Hotel bellhop: minimum of $2 or as a rule $1 per bag

Hotel housekeeper: $2 to $5 per night

*Hotel doorman: $1 per bag or $1
per person for hailing a cab*

*Hairstylist: 15 to 20 percent of service bill
(excluding hair products purchased)*

Shampoo person: $2

Manicurist, masseuse, or esthetician:
15 to 20 percent of service bill

⌁ Faux Pas in Foreign Countries ⌁

When you are traveling abroad, it's a great idea to research manners and customs before visiting. Doing this helps you avoid any major faux pas while you're away. Of course, you are not guaranteed against causing a cultural offense, but at least you can try. I am telling you this from experience. With all of the traveling I have done, I have committed a litany of faux pas, simply from being uninformed. When visiting a temple in Sri Lanka, I had to borrow a shawl to cover my tank top–clad shoulders. When dining in France, I did not know that it is rude to keep your hands under the table while dining there, that you should keep your hands visible at all times. When meeting my in-laws in their English countryside house for the first time, I immediately removed my shoes as I was accustomed to doing in California, then felt very awkward as I was the only one who wandered around barefoot. When visiting a drugstore in Spain, I was reprimanded by the clerk for actually reaching for a product on the shelf. He said he would get it for me. Shall I go on? Clearly, I have a lot to learn! The best advice is not to get defensive when you are corrected. When visiting a foreign country, you should abide by their rules. If you don't like their rules, just let that make you grateful for where you live.

⏤ Plane Etiquette ⏤

Flying can be stressful enough. Employ good airplane etiquette to help your trip go as smoothly as possible:

Dress nicely for air travel. You don't want to be one of those people wandering around the terminal in your pajamas. You can be comfortable and still look chic by choosing loose-fitting clothing in soft fabrics. Who knows? You might be promoted to first class.

Be prepared when going through security. You know

what's going to happen, so get everything ready. Be prepared to take off your shoes and your belt. Be prepared to put your laptop in the tray provided, empty your pockets, and dispose of any liquids that are not allowed. This helps the line flow faster.

Don't try to sneak full-sized luggage into the overhead bin.

Greet your seatmates and engage in polite conversation, but do not monopolize their flight by talking to them the entire time.

If you are going to put your seat back, be aware of the person behind you. Never do this while their tray is down and they are eating.

Avoid monopolizing the armrests. It is polite to give the armrests to the person in the middle seat.

Never wear a strong fragrance when traveling, as it might make fellow passengers nauseous.

When disembarking the plane, let everyone in front of you exit first.

Be patient. At some point in your air-travel experience, it is highly likely you will face a delay. Just breathe deeply and remember that some things are out of your power. Keep your good manners even when everyone else is yelling at the airline representative.

Public Transport Etiquette

On escalators stand to the right and walk on the left.

Always let passengers exit before you enter.

Always offer your seat to elderly people, disabled people, or pregnant ladies.

Avoid talking loudly on your cell phone. When engaging in conversation with another passenger, speak quietly and never curse.

Never put your feet up on a seat.

Never do personal grooming in a public place (no hair brushing, nail clipping, makeup sessions, etc.)

Never place your bag on a seat and force another passenger to stand.

Have your ticket or fare ready.

Do not eat food while in transit.

If you sneeze, do so into your arm or hankie. Make sure it is well away from any passengers.

Never block the door as passengers try to exit. Step out briefly, allow them to exit, and then hop back on.

Your poise is much needed in this hectic and unmannerly world. Have comfort in your convictions even though they are not always easy to uphold.

Chapter 10

NOT JUST A PRETTY FACE

Okay, now we look great, we've got killer posture, we can communicate gracefully (most of the time), we've polished our table manners, and we have made our homes suitable for living with poise. Now it's time to take it a step further. We are so much more than our pretty faces and stylish clothes. We are more than our mannerisms and the way we carry ourselves. We are more than the way we keep our homes and eat our meals. To fully develop our inner chic as well, we need to cultivate our intelligence, shift our perspectives, and be of service to others.

✑ Cultivate Your Intelligence ✑

It is difficult not to get caught up in the dumbing down of society. Popular culture makes it so hard for us. Mind-numbing reality television shows starring shallow men and women who have misplaced priorities and hot tempers are offered on so many channels. So many mainstream movies seem to be rife with either lowbrow humor or never-ending robot explosions. Popular music is polluted with shocking lyrics that are better suited for the gutter. Entertainment news lauds celebrities not for their talent but for their outrageousness. Yes, it is quite easy to get hypnotized by this lowbrow culture. For me also.

Cultivating your intelligence starts with choosing what you view and listen to. It doesn't mean you can't go see the summer blockbuster that everyone is talking about, but it does mean that you also seek out that independent theater show-ing the foreign film you heard so many good things about. It doesn't mean you can't watch reality TV again, but that you also find the shows that are more enriching. You might have to search a little harder to find pop music that croons beauti-ful instead of dirty lyrics, but you can find it, because those artists are out there and are worthy of our attention.

Perhaps you were passionate about a musician, an art-ist, or a writer when you were in school, but you have let the harsh reality of work, marriage, mortgages, and kids smother that fiery passion you had. Start by getting interested in a new topic. It could be art or politics. It could be history or inter-war English novels. It could be learning a new skill such as knitting or playing an instrument. It could be taking a French class again after all these years. It could be reading that Dick-ens novel you always wanted to read or attending your local Shakespeare festival. It could be studying the works of Cho-pin by reading about his life and listening to his music.

This is chic. This is poise. Refining all aspects of your life for the well-being of yourself and others. You will have so much to talk about at the next party you attend. You'll inspire others to look into what you're passionate about. Your viewers will appreciate you for reminding them that they used to have a passion for topics like these as well.

If you are a young person and find yourself passionate about a topic right now, never let go of that passion for learning. Find the field you are interested in and delve deeply there. Indulge your interest in studying Russian architecture. Keep practicing that piano. Champion your favorite musicians and let them know you appreciate their art. Cultivate your mind and in doing so cultivate your poise so you are not just a pretty face, but a smart one too.

RESOURCES FOR CULTIVATING YOUR MIND

www.kusc.org: Classical KUSC is a listener-supported classical radio station that also streams online. They have opera shows, symphony broadcasts, and many other musical treats, great for the classical connoisseur in you.

www.npr.org: Check out NPR online, particularly their Arts & Life section, which discusses books, movies, popular culture, food, art, design, performing arts, and photography.

www.getty.edu: The Getty Museum website offers a virtual online library where you can read and download Getty publications for free.

www.ted.com and www.tedxtalks.ted.com: TED and TEDx talks are about ideas worth spreading. You can find fun and informative lectures on nearly every subject under the sun given by dynamic and diverse speakers.

iTunes U: Listen to university lectures from the most renowned colleges around the world for free on iTunes U.

TELEVISION SHOWS WITH POISE

Keeping Up Appearances: Hyacinth Bucket, the show's protagonist, aims to rise above her family's slovenly mannerisms to be poised, elegant, and the toast of society but has so many mishaps along the way. This hilarious farce is legendary in television history.

Murder, She Wrote: If you are a mystery buff like me, you will appreciate how Jessica Fletcher handles the most perilous situations. Appropriately dressed and looking presentable always, Mrs. Fletcher solves crime after crime (after crime) with elegance, intelligence, and grace.

Cedar Cove: Judge Olivia Lockhart, played by Andie MacDowell, is the epitome of modern elegance and poise in this pleasant series from the Hallmark Channel.

Downton Abbey: Check out this wildly popular period drama and observe how poise can be found both above and below the stairs.

I Love Lucy: Lucy Ricardo is always getting into trouble, but she does it in style. While Lucy might often have been the butt of the joke, she sure had class.

Agatha Christie's Poirot: David Suchet brings Christie's most famous character, Hercule Poirot, to life in a way that would have made Christie so proud. Sure this Belgian detective had his quirks, but no one could deny that he had poise.

Mapp & Lucia: Whether you watch the 1985 or 2014 version of this classic comedy of manners, revel in the level of poise that Mapp and Lucia emit while climbing the social ladder of Tilling society.

MOVIES WITH POISE

Alice in Wonderland (1951): Alice employs her manners and poise even while chasing the white rabbit, being insulted by flower beds, and outwitting the Queen of Hearts in this Disney classic.

My Fair Lady (1964): Eliza Doolittle's miraculous transformation affirms that it doesn't matter who you are or where you come from, you too can have poise.

Gigi (1958): In this quintessential coming-of-age story, Gigi transforms herself from a boisterous and unruly girl to a graceful woman.

Top Hat (1935): In this unlikely romance, a comedy of errors erupts. But oh, how gracefully do Fred Astaire and Ginger Rogers dance? Their level of poise is inspirational.

To Catch a Thief (1955): This suspenseful Hitchcock thriller shows that even a reformed cat burglar can have class. Be inspired by Grace Kelly and Cary Grant's elegant and exciting embodiment of poise on the French Riviera.

Take Pride in Everything You Do

You might not be living your dream life right now, but if you're serious about cultivating poise, you must change your perspective. Take pride in absolutely everything you do. Cleaning house. Filing those spreadsheets at work. Ironing your clothes. Dealing with that customer who walks through the door just as you're about to close the shop. Cleaning the pots in your kitchen. Volunteering at your community's spring fair. Take pride in what you do. Give it your all. Give it your full attention. Madame Chic took pride in everything that she did. She didn't waste time griping about her lot in life. If she wanted to be doing something other than what she was doing, I would not have known.

Sure you might be waiting tables when you'd rather be starring in movies, but that doesn't mean you should approach your waitress job with disdain. Gratitude is key here. Be grateful to have a job and make sure you give that job your absolute best effort. Take pride in it. No experience is wasted. Poised people understand that doing something well helps you stand out. It draws attention to your excellence and will open doors for you that you never even knew were there.

In a 2009 blog post on the *Sartorialist*, blogger Scott Schuman profiled his driver in San Francisco. He wrote this:

One of my favorite encounters on this book tour was my driver in San Francisco.

As you can see he was very elegant and practically

oozed self-confidence, dignity and pride in his work. I love people who show pride in their work, regardless of the job.

This man's car was spotless, his shoes were shined and he knew exactly where he was going. He wasn't dressed like that for me, he had no idea who I was, this was just another day and just another ride done in his own stylish way.

I've said this so many times before, and recently in the intro of my book. Even though this blog is about fashion I don't really think about fashion when I look at this photo. I think about how he is communicating his sense of pride and self-worth; not by how expensive his clothes are but by how he wears his clothes, his posture and his politeness. This man is pure style.

Now, it could be that Mr. Schuman's driver was doing his dream job, or it could be that he had other ambitions. Either way, this driver had committed to taking pride in his job, and he professed that with his appearance and his demeanor. Poised people embrace reality. There is no use being in denial. If your reality is to clean up the kitchen at the end of the day, no fairy godmother is going to do it for you. Rather than sulking while you work, take pride in it. Give it your best and do it with style. Try to have a positive attitude in everything that you do. You will find yourself less distracted, more satisfied, and more able to appreciate the simple pleasures in life.

∼ Managing Expectations ∼

> Blessed is he who expects nothing, for
> he shall never be disappointed.
>
> —Alexander Pope

Are you a perfectionist? When things don't go your way, are you surprised? Do you often find yourself feeling disappointed? As we develop poise, we also need to manage our expectations. Poised people are ready for whatever comes their way, and when things don't go their way, they adjust their perspective and trust that every situation in life can be meaningful.

When I was invited to New York to give a TEDx talk on the ten-item wardrobe, I could not have been more excited. Giving a TEDx talk was a dream of mine, and now I was actually going to do it! I didn't hesitate to accept and booked my flight from California and my hotel in Manhattan as soon as the talk was confirmed.

After seeing so many TED talks on the internet, I definitely had high expectations of how mine would go. I pictured myself on a state-of-the-art stage with the latest sound technology, a large audience filling the plush seats before me, and the magnificent TEDx logo sign glowing behind me as I delivered my talk.

When I took the car from my hotel in Manhattan to Staten Island the day before the talk, to attend the rehearsal, I was surprised by the venue. The talks were not going to be delivered in a state-of-the-art theater but in a bar. Yes, you read that correctly, a bar. The kind of bar you went to in college. Black floors, walls, and ceilings, complete with bumper stickers in the bathroom and a dartboard in the hall. Hmm. This wasn't what I had pictured. The stage area was small but promising. There were professional theater lights.

Presumably bands played here on the weekends. There was even a room offstage that could act as a green room. Okay, so this wasn't perfect, but I could work with it. I decided to reserve judgment and see what rehearsal was like. But nearly an hour passed after the rehearsal was set to begin, and we had not yet heard from the event organizers. The speakers were all getting to know one another, and only a few people seemed to be bothered by the casualness of the rehearsal. I started to get frustrated. My expectations were not being met. This was not the affair I had pictured. I had so many questions.

When the organizers arrived, I accosted one of them and bombarded him with queries, the first being what the speaking order was for the next day. He had few answers for me. I went back to the hotel that night frustrated, not even knowing if I was going to be giving my talk in the morning or the late afternoon.

It ended up being a wonderful event; it all came together at the last minute. Sure, it wasn't the chicest of venues, but some incredible talks were delivered that day. Some very passionate ideas were shared and some very moving performances were given. I was proud to have been a part of it. But, most important, I learned the big lesson that I needed to manage my expectations. That no matter what the circumstances, I could still deliver the best talk of my life. It didn't matter if I was on a small stage surrounded by an atmosphere that was less than state-of-the-art. It didn't matter that my vision of a perfect event didn't match that of the organizers. All that mattered was that I deliver my heart that day and connect with the audience in a meaningful way.

So if you find yourself in what you think are less than ideal circumstances, surrounded by people who are not doing things "your way," don't get dejected. Ask yourself why you are in this situation and what lessons you can learn from it. See if you can change your perspective. I was expecting a TED-talk caliber production, but TEDx talks are local, grassroots productions, and therein lies their beauty. I learned that day to let go of my need for perfection. I learned how important it was to be there as a support for other people and to lift people up with praise. I learned that I could have delivered that talk standing in a landfill and still have gotten my point across. So when you are in situations that are not up to your standards, don't judge and don't dismiss them. Be the light you need to be for others. Get rid of your expectations, because regardless of how you think something should go, *you are not there by accident.* If you think this way, no experience of yours will be wasted.

Thinking of others

We are so often thinking of ourselves: what *we* want, what *we* need, where *we* want to go, and what *we* want to do. A poised person knows that extending grace to others is one of the most rewarding things you can do. Madame Chic regularly volunteered at her church and made that an integral part of her life.

Get involved with a community or an organization that helps other people. Volunteer your time and your resources to make the world a better place for someone else. If you feel stuck or in a rut, get out there and help other people. We must see what we can bring to the occasion, not what we can get out of it. By doing even the smallest act of service for another you are being a part of something big. In the same way it is more gratifying to listen than to speak, it is also so much more enjoyable to give than to receive. Commit to serving others; it's the poised thing to do because it lifts us out of our problems and allows us to look at the world from another person's perspective.

Poise is about so much more than looking presentable and behaving properly. It's also about cultivating a depth of character that comes from keeping our minds sharp, taking pride in everything we do, and serving others. When we commit to bettering ourselves on a deeper level, our daily experiences become more meaningful. Our inner chic is cultivated, and it radiates from the inside out in the most beautiful way.

Chapter 11

POISE AND *LES AUTRES*

> If you think you're enlightened, go
> spend a week with your family.
>
> —Ram Dass

We can cultivate poise from the comfort of our homes, where few challenges test us. Our homes are safe, after all. While we are at home, we run the show. But what happens when we throw other people in the mix, like coworkers, extended family, strangers, and neighbors? We must be prepared to deal with other people in a gracious and poised manner no matter how they behave toward us. This might sound easier than it is, but if we arm ourselves with the poised perspective, anything is possible.

⟨ *L'enfer, C'est les Autres?* ⟩

French philosopher Jean-Paul Sartre's most famous line in his play *No Exit* was "*L'enfer, c'est les autres,*" which translates as "Hell is other people." I went around agreeing with this sentiment for a large portion of my life. Gosh, other people can be difficult. Whenever I would have a heated encounter with someone, whether it was my husband or a stranger, I would always say to myself, "*L'enfer, c'est les autres!*" I would blame the other person for the small "hell" I was experiencing in dealing with them. But I now know that the hell Sartre is referring to is not other people. It is created by us—by our perspective when we are dealing with others. Once I came to realize this, I ceased to allow my happiness to be ruled by other people's actions.

The poised person takes responsibility for her actions and does not blame others or make excuses for her unhappiness. Sometimes all it takes is a little change of perspective.

That's an interesting perspective

If you live with or near other people, you will inevitably be annoyed by something they do. Whether it's a spouse, roommate, or neighbor, it's going to happen. Hey, even our children can annoy us. You might be arguing with your husband over a money issue. Your coworker might eat the sandwich you put in the office fridge (again!), the one that even had your name on it. Your children might completely ignore you while you announce it's bath time. These things can trigger something in us. We might not fly off the handle immediately, but over time, when they keep happening, we want to explode.

Whenever you feel self-righteous in anger, ask yourself if you can look at the situation from a different perspective. This trick does many things: it allows you to pause before acting; it prompts you to question your thoughts to see if you are blowing the issue out of proportion; and it gives you clarity to take the best course of action. Most important, it calms you down. That calmness—choosing peace—is part of the poise that we are striving for.

More on perspective

My oldest daughter went through a phase where she cried every morning after waking up. I think she was frustrated and couldn't voice what it was that she needed, so she just cried. The rest of us would be slumbering, and at 6 a.m. I would hear a loud wailing from the girls' room. I would always go in there and soothe her, but believe me her waking up like that was enough to make me want to cry too. We were all so frustrated. I would sit on the edge of her toddler bed, trying to talk to her about it. Finally, I realized that I should show her a different perspective. I said to her, "You know, it doesn't have to be like this. You can wake up in the morning and feel happy." When I said this to her, her little three-year-old face lit up. (This could very well have been her first major aha! moment.) She repeated, "It doesn't have to be like this?" "No," I said, smiling. "You can wake up and choose to be happy. If you need to go to the bathroom, you can go. If you need a glass of water, you can drink from the one on your nightstand. If you want to play with your dolls, you can do that. If you need to talk to Mom and Dad, you can come into our room. Or you can lie in your bed and think about the day ahead. You can think of your friends. You can say a prayer. You can be happy!"

It was as though my showing her a different perspective on the morning was giving her permission to enjoy the morning. She doesn't wake up screaming anymore. And she is also sleeping a lot later. Magic? Perhaps. Changing one's perspective is like magic because it opens up a whole new world you didn't even know existed.

⫯⟋ Non-poised People ⟍⫯

Whether you already practice many of the concepts in this book, or you've just started the journey, after reading the book you will probably begin to notice the shortcomings of other people's poise. This could be a blessing or a curse, depending on how you look at it. You might find yourself in situations where other people are hopelessly clueless in this area, and it might irritate you.

You might feel frustrated with how the parents at your children's Christmas play chat loudly in the audience after their child's part is over, just as your child is taking the stage. At work you might feel annoyed by the customer who walks up to you and barks a question without greeting you first. You might feel irritated by the neighbor who completely ignores you as you pass each other in the stairwell every morning. You might feel judgmental about the lady who is wearing her pajamas to the post office or the man on the bus with the offensive image on his T-shirt. It's important that we don't judge these people negatively and dismiss them completely as lost causes. We must be extra courteous to them and remember to use our manners and employ patience. This is not to suggest that you allow people to take advantage of you. You can ask the people talking during the play to please be quiet. You can take the time to greet the rude customer before you answer his or her question. You can still say "good morning" to the neighbor who ignores you on a regular basis. Instead of giving up in despair, look at it like this: *You are needed there. They need you to shine your light on them. They are your viewers, whether they know it or not, and you have the opportunity to provide a good example of poise for them.*

You see, many people have never had good role models. They've never known anything different. You can be a role model. You might never see the fruits of your efforts. You might never know how your behavior has affected someone. And that's okay. Even if just one person is inspired to slow down and lead a more intentional life because of your example, you have done a great service to this person. So rather than looking at being in the company of un-poised people as a curse, look at it as a blessing. This is your opportunity to shine your light and be of service. You are needed now more than ever.

❧ Choose Your Friends Wisely ❧

> He who walks with the wise grows
> wise, but a companion of fools suffers
> harm.
>
> —Proverbs 13:20

As you cultivate the art of poise, you might notice your friendships change. Your friends might act differently toward you, or you might notice something different in them. Don't cut off a friend just because she isn't cultivating poise like you are. Let's not get dramatic here. It is a good idea, however, to assess your friendships and perhaps forge a new one with someone who shares your newfound values, priorities, and passions.

Seek out friends who have common goals and interests, and your journey to cultivate poise will become so much more delightful.

One of the things I love about my blog is that it gives me the chance to see a community of women coming together, excited about living a refined life. Many of them say the only place they can find like-minded people is on the *Daily*

Connoisseur blog! So seek out those like-minded friends, and with regard to your friends who aren't quite there yet, unless they are dabbling in highly questionable behavior, be patient with them. Your poise might rub off on them. You might be in their life for this very reason.

Difficult Times

When I lived in Paris and was immersed in an exciting new world, cultivating poise was quite effortless for me. The environment was so accommodating. Times were good! When sitting at a café with my friends with not a care in the world, I found it easy to focus on good posture and being gracious and graceful. When my biggest care was whether to walk down the Champs Élysées or venture through the Jardin des Tuileries, it was easy for me to work on my elegant bearing. When the only drag in my day was having to do an hour or two of homework, it was easy to maintain a positive attitude.

But what about during the difficult times? What about when real life takes over? What about when you're into hour seven of your waitressing shift and you get another rude customer? What about when the rent is due and you're not sure how you're going to pay it? What about when you and your husband keep disagreeing over a parenting issue? What about when one of your children is going through a phase that tests you at every turn? What about when you have an hour commute each way and you feel as though you couldn't possibly sit in traffic for one more minute? It is challenging to maintain your poise during difficult times, but it is even *more critical* that you maintain it at such times. Just as how you live behind closed doors reveals how you live your entire life, how you maintain (or not maintain) poise during difficult moments is a true test of your conviction. When you are in the midst of difficult times, poise is the first thing you'd like to get rid of. And it's often the first thing to go. You will fight with your husband and say something unkind to him. You will snap and scream at your child. You'll experience road rage on your commute. You'll lose hope. What is the point of poise when everything looks so bleak?

During those difficult moments, when you feel as though your poise is going to go out the window, pause. Take a deep breath. Don't feel the need to speak right away. Silence here is powerful. Don't clench your jaw. Keep your head high. No trial is too daunting. You can and you will get through these difficult times. Nothing, not even a bad thing, lasts forever. A true test is how you choose to get through it.

Even though you know the difficult times won't last forever, the poised person also knows that no moment is wasted. Once you shift your perspective, you will realize there is a silver lining in all trials; you will actually become grateful for the difficult moments. You will see that these trials only make you stronger and increase your resolve. Be thankful for the difficult people in your life, for they are teaching you assertiveness and tolerance. Be grateful for the job you didn't get or the person who dumped you, because guess what? There is probably something or someone better out there for you. Change your perspective in the difficult times. Get through each situation and take what lessons you can from it. These difficult times are building your character and strengthening your poise. That is not to say that these dark times won't be challenging. *Pas du tout.* They will be an immense challenge, but you will come out of them stronger than you were before.

∾ Good Times ∾

Ah, we finally get to the fun part. Poise in good times is not only easier but exceptionally more enjoyable. It makes the good times even better. When everyone is getting along, when things are going your way, when you are enjoying life— you will hit these pockets of perfection in life, when you burst with happiness and contentment. Your project gets picked up at work. You get a promotion. You have an amazing first date. You are celebrating a milestone anniversary. You win the writing competition. You score the grant. You watch your children dancing and laughing in the backyard. During the good times, the most important thing is to remain grateful and humble. Poised people don't take things for granted, and they don't brag about what they have.

During the good times remain deliciously in the present moment. Give yourself permission to enjoy life! It doesn't always have to be a struggle. Remember that good times, just like the bad, are also temporary. Our days, our relationships, our lives are fluid entities that can swiftly change from one moment to the next. We must delight in the good times and be equally prepared for the bad. We do not want to be these emotional pendulums that sway with the current situation and are only happy when things go our way. Poised people have rock-solid understanding that life has its twists and turns. They look at it all like a delicious adventure and a sporting challenge, one they wholeheartedly accept.

Poised as a Way of Life

We come to the close of this book. But we do not come to a close on our journey of cultivating poise. In fact, it's only just begun. No matter where you begin, whether you are a complete novice to living a poised life or consider yourself a seasoned veteran, you can benefit from committing to be your best self each day, from the moment you get up to the moment you lie down for sleep. Keep your mind sharp and your skills relevant. Adorn your body beautifully and carry yourself through this messy life with grace and elegance. Maintain your integrity no matter whom or what you encounter.

You might be the only one in your family who cares about deportment. You might be the only one among all of your friends who speaks without swearing. You might be the only person on your block who dresses up on a daily basis. You might feel lonely in your endeavors. It might seem like a waste of time. *But never give up.* Because you are the light for all of the darkness you encounter each day. You and you alone can be the catalyst for change that another soul dearly needs. You and you alone can make others want to be better. You and you alone can give hope. Just when people are ready to resign, they can see you and the way you live and be intrigued by it. Your passion for life, your commitment to persevering is so attractive. It is so rare. You are not striving for perfection. You continue to be very much imperfect, but you are going to give it your all because you have viewers and *you matter*.

See the sheer beauty of cultivating poise as a way of life. It will be hard, but it will be an adventure. Life will never be dull. Every moment in every day will be a challenge. You will be required to question yourself at every turn and to strive always for the highest choice. You will go through many failures and you will never be perfect. But you will be living a very fulfilling life. Your efforts will matter dearly.

Don't allow the ways of the world to discourage you. Let them motivate you to shine even more brightly. Yes, you will stand out. It might feel uncomfortable at first. You might be misunderstood. But you will make a difference to *someone*. And that is all that matters. So roll up your sleeves and get ready to put in some hard work. Get ready to cultivate the art of poise and get ready to change your life. Because *your life alone can change the world*.

ACKNOWLEDGMENTS

My deepest gratitude goes to my agent, Erica Silverman, and my editor, Trish Todd. Thank you for your friendship and your belief in my work. I am so happy we found each other. Team Chic! Thank you to the very talented teams at Trident Media Group and Simon & Schuster, with special thanks to Lauren Paverman, Meredith Miller, Tara Carberry, Kaitlin Olson, Jackie Seow, and Jonathan Karp. Thank you to Virginia Johnson for your oh-so-chic illustrations. Sincere thanks go to the readers and viewers of my blog, *The Daily Connoisseur*, as well as the Madame Chic fans all around the world. Thank you to my fabulous friends for keeping me passionate. Thank you to my family for your support and encouragement. And lastly, my biggest thank-you goes to Ben, Arabella, and Georgina. You inspire me every day. I love you dearly.

ABOUT THE AUTHOR

Jennifer L. Scott is the *New York Times* best-selling author of *Lessons from Madame Chic* and *At Home with Madame Chic* (Simon & Schuster) and creator of the blog *The Daily Connoisseur*. She is a contributing writer for *Huffington Post Style* and has been featured on CNN, BBC, and CBS News, and in the *New York Times*, *Vanity Fair*, *USA Today*, *Newsweek*, and the *Daily Mail*. She lives with her family in Los Angeles, California.